The Friendly School

The Friendly School

A Front Office Guide to

Excellent Customer Service

Jeff Nash

www.schoolcustomerservice.org

This book is dedicated to all of our hard-working public servants – who willingly sacrifice for the sake of children and families in our respective communities.

Thank you for your service!

Table of Contents

FOREWORD

I have enjoyed the good fortune of working with many awe-inspiring co-workers throughout my career. When I reflect on those who were the most effective school people, I never consider who was most knowledgeable, most talented, most energetic, most educated or even most professional.

Nope. The people who were most effective have always been those most skilled in building relationships. I believe that is the secret sauce for great schools. Relationships are indeed the foundation for learning.

Over the years, I have spent considerable time trying to figure out if relationship skills are instinctive or learned. After all, I don't recall a single high school or college course focused on the art of relationships.

In every school district, and at every level, there are staff members who are incredibly eloquent in their work with students, parents and colleagues. Unfortunately, every school district also has staff members who would be better suited for less interactive jobs.

Jeff Nash is one of those people who stands out as a specialist in building and maintaining relationships. In fact, his skills in this area are unrivaled. I have seen firsthand how he relates with people of all ages, backgrounds and education levels. Jeff makes a great first impression, and goes to great lengths to ensure everyone around him feels both welcomed and valued.

I can think of no better person to write a guide for excellent school customer service. Jeff has served as a teacher, department chair, basketball coach, school administrator, central office administrator and right hand to the superintendent. His perspective is one that considers the entire community.

I am privileged to call Jeff a friend...and it is with full confidence that I highly recommend this book for all educators – particularly for those who work in the offices of our schools and districts.

- Dr. Rydell Harrison

INTRODUCTION

Hello and welcome. My name is Jeff Nash and I have the good fortune of serving as President of the American Association of School Customer Service.

There are plenty of customer service books out on the market. Thank you for choosing this one. I am a school person and have written **The Friendly School** specifically for school people...a very special breed!

The value of the information provided in this book is in its relevance to the specific everyday challenges of SCHOOL personnel. As we know, customer service is very different in schools than it is in the corporate world. A business may gauge the quality of its service based upon upselling, reselling or some other profit measure. However, it is much harder to determine the success of school service. After all, how do we really know if the service we offer is effective? Great question.

I will try to answer this question, and many more, as we journey through this book together. In fact, I may raise a few questions for you regarding your personal service habits. You have been warned!

About twenty years ago, I started teaching customer service classes to co-workers in my own school district. Along the way, I have enjoyed the good fortune of working with tens of thousands of amazing school folks throughout North America. I have learned a lot from them, including the conflict many of our decision-makers face regarding customer service improvement. On the one hand, it seems most superintendents, principals and other leaders believe that their schools or districts are in need of a tune up, and they want their staff – especially their office staff – to participate in customer service training. On the other hand, they are hesitant to send their staff to training because the leaders know the school or office tends to get chaotic when staff members are away from the building. They are excited to send them, but too chicken to have them gone. What is an excited chicken to do? A dilemma indeed.

I believe *The Friendly School* provides a workable solution. I will be the first to tell you that the best learning experience is the one that includes a live instructor. I love live training events, and after all these years it is still a privilege to teach those classes. The ability to ask questions and participate in class discussions is invaluable. While this book is not an appropriate substitute for a live class, or even for a great online class, it can be a great tool to provide insights and practical tips to both tighten up and enhance your customer service offerings.

It is my intent that this book helps you in three distinct ways:

First, it will lay a theoretical foundation for why customer service is a school issue. I realize this sounds incredibly boring, but most of us would agree customer service is important, and therefore, this topic is necessary to discuss. Unfortunately, as the old saying goes – common courtesy is not always common practice.

Second, you will come away with a much greater understanding of why we should – and how we can – invest in our customer service habits PRIOR to engaging with a customer.

Much of our customer service impact is directly determined by what we do PRIOR to the start of our customer interaction. Too often, it is the pre-interaction work that gets short-changed. Yet, with a few small tweaks in this area, our service can be noticeably better and friendlier. Hence...*The Friendly School*.

Finally, you will find a multitude of practical tips among these pages. My goal for you is to identify at least three tips that you will bring to your work and begin implementing immediately. I want this book to assist you in your pursuit to provide world-class customer service to your students, staff, parents, and community.

Thank you again for allowing my thoughts and ideas regarding customer service to be a small part of your regular work habits. I am truly humbled. Happy reading!

Chapter 1: Know Your Audience

You may have heard it said, when speaking to a group, we should know our audience. Likewise, as an author, I should know my readers. Experience has taught me a good bit about the folks who might read a book like *The Friendly School*. For the most part, readers can be filtered into one of three easily distinguishable buckets.

Prisoners

Occasionally, people read a book like this or take a customer service class because they are, well, prisoners. Someone is making them do it. Prisoners are very easy to spot in a live training event because their gestures give them away. You may find them sitting with their arms crossed, frequently glancing at their watches or, if they can get away with it, engaging in a conversation via their cell phones.

1

True story, one time while we were conducting a customer service training class, a guy turned his chair around so his back was to the trainer and sat that way for three whole hours! During that time, we found no humor in his behavior. In fact, it took all of our strength not to feel personally offended. The funny part, however, occurred after the training, when he made it a point to let us know how much he actually enjoyed the class. Fascinating! It turns out he was not mad at us but was angry with the supervisor who mandated his attendance.

If you are reading this book as a prisoner, I hope you will somehow, someway, find enjoyment in these pages. I also hope that you will specifically seek out at least three nuggets that you can take back to your everyday service habits...three tips that will help you in your future customer interactions. Perhaps those will be small practical tips, or maybe some large theoretical paradigm shifts. Either way, be on the lookout for those golden nuggets.

Tourists

Some of our readers are tourists – always ready to "get away from it all." They may or may not have interest in this topic, but reading this book is better (or less bad) than whatever else they would be otherwise doing. I can easily identify the tourists in live training events because they are the people with the least amount of stress. They are simply glad to be participating in any activity, as long as they are not in their offices.

As with the prisoners, the same thing applies to any tourists reading this book: I hope you will find those three nuggets that you can take back to your everyday service habits.

Learners

The final group is simply referred to as the learners. These folks see a topic of interest, and decide they want to learn more about it. They may have a natural curiosity about the subject. In some cases, if competitive by nature, they are concerned that someone else may be learning something that they don't know, and they want to know what it is. In live training events, trainers love these folks because they ask most of the questions and help stimulate the class conversation.

If you are reading as a learner, thank you for your interest. I hope it will be worth your while. Find your three golden nuggets.

Now, whether you are reading this book as a prisoner, a tourist, or as a learner, I believe it will provoke new thinking about your approach to customer interactions, and it will challenge your existing customer service habits. For that to happen, you will have to be willing to take a very honest and humble look at yourself. This could get a little painful. Self-assessment is not for the easily offended.

Of course, if you have worked in a school or school district for any length of time, you have already developed a skin thick enough to handle anything I can throw your way.

Ultimately, I believe you will find it fun, helpful and rewarding as you invest in your approach to customer interactions from this point forward.

Proceed to the next chapter if you dare!

Chapter 2: Goals

Let's begin our journey by identifying a handful of simple goals for providing great customer service. These are not listed in any order of importance and, in fact, you may find it a useful exercise to assign value to each – and then list them in priority order. It is my expectation that these goals will provide a framework for recognizing and achieving great service levels.

Identify Your Customers and Their Needs

We will define two distinct types of customers, then we will examine the fundamental needs that are applicable to all customers. If we meet these needs, we will have very happy people with very few complaints.

Recognize Causes of Bad Service

Bad service is always entertaining to talk about because we all have great stories of times when we have received bad service. You should, however, challenge yourselves to consider times when you have been the one offering bad service...ouch!

Acknowledge Common Shortfalls

In our practice, we frequently uncover universal shortfalls, so we might as well call attention to them. If we are honest with ourselves, we probably have perpetuated these shortfalls at some point. Identifying them is the best start to eliminating them.

List Practical Tips for Good Service

I will highlight four specific modes of service. Fair warning, it is quite likely that you will not agree with all the tips I am going to share. Expect to find some of them more challenging than others, but you can choose which ones you are willing to implement into your everyday service habits. For the record, your critical analysis of these tips is a good sign of progress.

Examine the Roles of Multiculturalism in Customer Service

There are differences in customer expectations among sub-groups, and we should be well-equipped to serve a diverse customer base. It is not enough to simply "play it safe" by not offending our customers who hail from cultures different than those with which we are comfortable. No, we need to meet them where they are – as uncomfortable as that may feel – and offer them the same great service as everyone else.

Preparing to Work with Difficult Customers

We have all experienced working with difficult customers – and, if we are honest, we have all likely been difficult customers ourselves! There are uncountable categories of difficult customers, each with unique personas, so I will discuss strategies to help us when we find ourselves interacting with them.

Draft Written Promise Statement

Probably not what you were expecting as a part of customer service, but I think you will see tremendous value in this discussion. This is not a very sophisticated document. It is a simple promise from your team to your customers. Your customers will appreciate a tangible, accountable promise.

Identify Positive First Impressions

Just a heads up, this eye-opening section may be a little more challenging than you expect.

Develop and Maintain a Favorable Reputation

A big part of customer service responsibilities is to manage not only your own professional reputation, but the reputation of your school, your department, and your school district. The consequences that accompany a reputation, favorable or unfavorable, are monumental. This book will discuss the ways to build and sustain a favorable reputation.

Practice Selling Your Organization

In advance of this section, you can be thinking about the "elevator speech" you would use to describe your school or district. The "elevator speech" is a concise sales pitch promoting the value of that organization. In an elevator speech you have about fifteen seconds to impress someone with regard to your school or district. What is the most important thing about your organization? What is it you want them to know?

Outline a Plan for Customer Service Revival

Near the end of this book, I will outline specific strategies you can implement to raise the bar for your entire organization.

There they are: the goals for our time together. Think you can handle it? If you can accomplish even one of these goals, your customers will appreciate your efforts.

Chapter 3: Defining Our Customers

School customer service is sometimes regarded as two foreign notions mixed together – customer service and schools. Why? Because customer service is traditionally considered a business concept. In my experience, I have had multiple school people express concerns with the term "customer service." They took issue with the word "customer." They insisted we don't have customers, we have constituents, we have clients, we have community, we have stakeholders, etc.

It was hard for me to share their angst. In fact, when it comes to the phrase "customer service," the focus should be on the service. If you would prefer not to call them customers, that's fine. But how are we serving these people? Please don't waste my time arguing semantics. Instead, tell me about your service. That's what matters.

It will be helpful to put all customers into one of two categories as we move through the book: *internal* customers and *external* customers. There are a variety of ways we could define these terms, but for the sake of creating a common language as we move through the rest of the book, I will define them as the following:

- *Internal* customers are going to be those who wear the same badge as you and work for the same employer. This category will include all of your co-workers as well as the employees from other buildings throughout your school district.

- *External* customers simply include everyone else...and that is a lot of people! Consider your students, their parents, community members, elected officials, media and even that grumpy guy who lives beside the school, frequently complaining about those noisy kids on the playground. These are all external customers.

On a personal note, my passion has always been geared for the external customer. Perhaps that is the PR guy in me. However, someone much wiser than me once offered some terrific advice when he cautioned, "Hey Jeff, watch out for your internal customers because they can ruin your day."

I didn't want to believe it. After all, internal customers are my co-workers. We are on the same team. Surely, they can't be that difficult, right? Well, if any of you work in your school district's human resources office, or perhaps your payroll office, you know the deal. Internal customers can undoubtedly be difficult if they are not appropriately served.

Lesson learned...the hard way!

Chapter 4: Pop Quiz

During our live sessions, I offer a pop quiz near the beginning of our time together. As you can guess, participants are usually pretty skeptical, but the good news is this quiz has no correct or incorrect responses. It consists of only two questions.

The first question simply asks for a number between 0 and 100. I ask everyone to consider all the people who work for their respective school districts – teachers, bus drivers, central office staff, guidance counselors, coaches, cafeteria, maintenance...everyone. Then, write the first number that comes to mind after they hear the following question:

What percent of people in your organization do not offer good customer service consistently?

Once they have written their answers to the first question, we proceed to the second question. This one gets a little more personal. The class is instructed to answer with only a "yes" or "no." They cannot offer a wishy washy safe answer like "sometimes" or "it depends."

You can probably guess the second question:

Do you offer good customer service consistently?

I publicly admit that the questions are not fair. Up until this point we have not yet defined two critical variables. The first variable is the word "good." We have not yet defined good service. Your idea of good service may be very different than someone else's idea of good service.

The second variable is "consistently." Some may think that calling a school and receiving good service (whatever that is) seven times out of ten is pretty consistent. Others may say nine times out of ten equals consistent.

The point is, without a standard definition of "good" or "consistent," the pop quiz questions can seem unfair. Nonetheless, there is a point to asking these questions.

Once they have finished writing their answers, I like to bring up two volunteers. I ask the first volunteer to head over to the chart paper and select a marker. Then I go around the class and ask each person to call out the number they wrote as their answer for question number one. The first volunteer records the numbers on the chart paper for us all to see. We typically find a pretty wide range in answers. As the classes are usually made up of people from the same school district, the wide range of numbers is rather eye-opening. Since participants are largely dealing with the same set of co-workers throughout the same school district, this tells us that *much of the customer experience is determined by the perception of the customer*. Interesting.

After the numbers are listed on the chart paper, I ask the second volunteer to grab a calculator, add up the numbers and divide by the number of people in the class in order to determine the average percentage. The results are often fascinating.

Upon using this quiz, a number of times, I began to realize that the average response for each class was always hovering right around 40%. Sometimes it was a few points higher, sometimes a few points lower, but almost always in the neighborhood of 37-43%.

I thought this phenomenon was specific to my own school district. Then one day, I was training a group of communication directors from school districts all across my state. Before class, I wondered how the pop quiz would play out. After all, these folks were answering question number one while considering their own colleagues from their own school districts, not all from the same district. Just for fun, prior to class, I wrote out a sign that read "37-43%" and kept it face down on the table. We then completed the quiz and calculated the class average. Wouldn't you know it...the class average was exactly 40%. The exact center of my predicted range. I then held up my pre-written sign for the class to see and they thought I was a genius...so did I!

What that really told me was the 40% watermark for school district personnel not offering good service consistently was not unique to my school district; it was a more universal trend. After using this quiz all over the country, I am comfortable telling you that I find the 40% number to be the nationwide consensus.

However, ask yourself this: Is it okay that 40% of your colleagues are not offering good service consistently? I hope you are shaking your head. In fact, I want you jumping on the table screaming emphatically, "No!" Of course, this is not acceptable. However, before you get too upset, we need to look at question number two.

The second question again is: Do *you* offer good customer service consistently? In our live training classes, I like to ask everyone who answered yes to question number two to raise their hand. Interestingly, in every class, almost every hand goes up. I have pondered the responses to this simple survey for years.

Why is it that we continue to identify roughly 40% of our teammates who do not offer good service consistently, but we all think that we – ourselves – offer good service consistently?

If 40% is accurate, then how come these people never come to my classes...or is it possible that 40% of the class is lying? I ask half kidding.

Asked another way, why is it that we see the customer service faults in our colleagues, but we don't see them in ourselves?

I believe – and have no research to back it up – the reason we notice the shortcomings in the service habits of others, but not in ourselves, can be attributed to the "good person syndrome." You see, we like to think of ourselves as good people. And since we think of ourselves as good people, therefore we must be good at customer service.

But herein lies the problem: Being a good person, while a nice foundation for customer service, does not equate to providing good service. By all accounts, Mother Teresa was a very good person. However, if she didn't return phone calls, she would have made a lousy customer service representative. Being a good person isn't exactly the same as being good at customer service, and that contributes significantly into the reason why we fail to readily see the pitfalls in our own service habits.

Chapter 5: Pet Peeves

We all have "buttons."

These buttons equate to certain habits, phrases, tones or gestures that simply get under our skin. Some are large, noticeable buttons, while others are small and unremarkable. We try to hide our annoyance, especially from our customers. But somehow, they always seem to find a way to push our buttons, don't they? Customers have a way of knowing just how to set us off.

In our live training, I ask participants to make a list of the behaviors that set them off. When we get to share our lists, someone in every class mentions how much they dislike when a customer talks down to us. Another common peeve is when a customer doesn't believe us, or asks to speak with our supervisor because they don't like the answer given — essentially answer shopping! Other popular peeves include customers reminding us that they are taxpayers who pay our salaries. That's always fun, right? Some of us lose our minds when a customer begins a sentence with "you people." I'll bet most just love it when a customer threatens to go to the press. Or how about when a customer wants to continue a conversation long after we have provided the necessary information? Perhaps our phone is ringing off the hook, people are lined up at the desk, and yet the customer wants to keep talking about mostly irrelevant things. Good times!

We could go further discussing our buttons, but a big part of improving customer service is getting ourselves to see our *own* customer service shortcomings. So, this time, what if we flipped the script? What if we were to ask a group of our customers to list *their* pet peeves – the things we do that drive them crazy, which push their buttons? What would they say?

Some of the more common customer pet peeves include us not returning phone calls, us not listening, us not looking or sounding professional, us using a tone that is anything other than friendly, and us sending written or typed responses that include spelling mistakes. There are others, certainly, but the point is this: It is easy to recognize the things our customers do that make us want to grind our teeth, but it is not always as easy to recognize the things *we* do that might drive our customers crazy.

It is important to remember that we cannot control our customer's behavior, but we can control our own. We must stop trying to "fix" our customers, and instead be on the lookout for ways we can clean up our own service. After all, the customer is not the professional, and is not required to behave in accordance with any pre-established set of rules (though common courtesy should come standard!).

If, after delivering service, you realize later that you in any way wronged or short-changed a customer, then be a professional and make it right. Whether that means offering a correction, an update, or even an apology, you can make it right. But if your customer wrongs you, try not to lose any sleep over it. Customers are not held to the same high standards as those who provide the service.

Chapter 6: Five Customer Needs

Of course, it would be naïve to believe there is a magic formula that will eliminate all customer dissatisfaction. However, if we, as customer service representatives, meet just a few basic needs, I propose we will have happier customers, with fewer problems, less escalation of problems – and a whole lot less customer drama.

In an earlier chapter we categorized all customers with one of two labels. They are either internal or external customers. Now, regardless of whether they are internal or external, all customers have basic, fundamental needs. We will identify a few of these needs below. Please feel free to add to the list. Keep in mind, these are not in any type of priority order.

Customers Need to Feel Welcome

This first need is simple, but not easy. Let me put this in plain terms — customers need to feel welcome. Now, you could put out a welcome mat and perhaps a little potpourri around your desk, but that's not really where we are going. The customer needs to feel welcome to approach you. Because we are school or district employees, and because our jobs are tax-funded, many customers will feel comfortable coming to you with a question or a need. They will feel comfortable coming to you...the first time. The real test for your welcoming skills is this: Do your customers feel comfortable coming to you a *second* time? If you are experiencing a lot of first-time customers, but no repeat customers, it might be time to examine your welcoming style. It's kind of like that great line from a classic movie, *The American President*. One of the lead characters, who was single, admitted she "seems to be having a lot of FIRST dates lately." Similarly, we should ask ourselves if we have given anyone reason to not want to approach us a second time or to not feel welcome around us.

Customers Need to Be Understood

The second universal need of all customers is to be understood. It is never the customer's responsibility to be understood; it is our job to understand. That is not always easy. Maybe the customer has an unfamiliar accent, or mannerisms that we do not recognize. Perhaps the customer uses different words that we are not accustomed to hearing. It took me three years of marriage to realize that when my wife, Lori, (born and raised in North Carolina) said she was "ill" that really, she was mad at me (born and raised in New York). I thought she needed an aspirin. Who knew?

If we are struggling to understand our customer, then we need to employ a different strategy. One strategy that seems to work well is to introduce the customer to a different person on the staff. It may be that the second staff member has a piece of information that could be helpful to the customer, or maybe has dealt with a similar situation recently. And once introduced to the customer, the initial representative is free to assist another customer.

I actually learned this strategy as a high school student working at a shoe store in the local mall. We were trained to never let the customer leave without buying a pair of shoes. Who sold the shoes did not matter as long as the customer made a purchase. If my approach was not working, and it looked like the customer was going to leave, it was my job to tactfully introduce a co-worker to the conversation. I realize it sounds like a greasy sales tactic, but it can be quite effective if done right – and customers get better service as a result.

Over the years, I have had boss-like conversations with multiple employees reminding them that it is not the customer's job to be understood – it is our job to understand.

Customers Need to Retain Dignity

The third universal customer need is to retain dignity. If you want to pour gasoline on a fire, then start talking down to your customers.

Always pay close attention to your tone and gestures. Be careful not to ask questions that may come off as condescending. It is important not to make customers feel like they have been dragged into the principal's office and scolded.

I can remember a season during my role as head of the school district's Welcome Center in which a strange phenomenon was occurring with increasing frequency.

You see, customers were supposed to sign in at the security desk, then come to the Welcome Center or another department if needed.

During this specific season, we had a security guard with the physique of a linebacker...and the heart of a missionary. When an angry customer returned to his station, instead of signing the customer out he would bring the customer to my office for assistance.

He would say something to the effect of, "Hey Jeff, she's having a rough time. Can you help her out?"

Upon delivering this angry customer to my office, my security guard friend then has to return to his station. What does one say to that? The customer is staring me down...red-faced and teary-eyed. I did not cause this situation, and likely do not have the authority to override whatever was told her by a different department. This is clearly not a five-minute solution. There is no escape. Buckle up...this is surely going to take at least a half hour.

So, of course, I would ask the only question I could think to ask, "Please, ma'am, tell me what happened."

Now, the interesting part of this story is that, for a season, I kept hearing the most remarkable descriptions from the customers. Their stories contained two very distinctive similarities. First, each customer's story involved the same administrator. I have to admit, she had a reputation for less than stellar customer service. Second, when they described the conversations, they each mentioned how she looked over her glasses when talking with (at) them.

Now as I get older, and being too cheap/stubborn to invest in bifocals, I admittedly find myself looking over my own glasses with greater frequency. But, in these complaints, the simple gesture of looking over the glasses, ACCOMPANIED BY A DEMEANING TONE, resulted in customers feeling as if their dignity had been hijacked. They repeatedly complained of being talked to as if they were somehow guilty.

Keep in mind, these customers were at our building because something was wrong in their lives. Ordinarily, they would have registered their children at school. However, because they did not have their own proof of residence – likely due to a divorce, foreclosure, eviction or some other unfortunate life event – they had to come to the central office. These parents, while often ashamed of their personal situations, were actually quite noble in that they were simply attempting to register their children for school. That's it...they were doing the right thing and got belittled for it! This should make your blood boil.

Our customers should leave our conversations with as much – or more – dignity than they had when they arrived.

Customers Need to Obtain Assistance

The fourth universal customer need is to obtain assistance. It is the main reason customers come to us in the first place. It may seem that you get asked the most stupid questions ever known to mankind, but it is imperative to give our customers the benefit of the doubt.

When we are in the middle of a weeklong snowstorm, and we have not been in school for the past three days and snow is still falling; we have sent home phone calls, email messages, updated the website, the district app, all social media accounts and alerted the press that there is no school tomorrow; you still get that person who asks you why his kid's bus is late.

We have to believe that they are not purposely trying to test our patience, but that they really just need help. They are not deliberately trying to steal our last ounce of sanity. They just need assistance.

In the end, show kindness – assist them with a smile.

Customers Need to Be Recognized as Valuable

A fifth universal customer need is to be recognized as valuable. This very well might be the easiest need to meet.

The absolute best customer service rep I ever met worked at the cleaners near my neighborhood. I believe she and her husband owned the store, but I never knew for sure because she could not speak English. Every once in a while, I would try to strike up a conversation, but she would smile and let me know she did not understand what I was saying.

Even though we did not share a common language, she mastered the art of customer service. She always smiled. She learned about me, knowing I liked my shirts heavily starched. She would see me coming in from the parking lot and have my shirts ready for me to pick up.

Her tone and gestures assured me of my value to her and to her business.

One day I was out running errands with my daughter and needed to pick up my shirts. I told my daughter, "Watch this. Your dad is a celebrity. They know me here."

We walked in to pick up my shirts and, to my surprise, my favorite customer service superstar totally ignored me in front of my daughter! Instead, she stared at my daughter for what seemed like an awkwardly long time. Then she broke into a huge smile and said one word – "Beautiful!"

Are you kidding? What a moment. I have no idea what she charged me for my laundry, but it did not matter. At that point I was a customer for life.

This lady had it figured out. She was spot on. All we have to do is convince our customers that we love their children, and will do everything we can to ensure their success, safety and happiness.

We do that, and they will walk through fire for our school or district...and give us the benefit of the doubt.

Chapter 7: Causes of Bad Service

What a fun topic! This is always one of my favorite parts of our training classes because it is never hard to find a volunteer to share a personal story about bad service. The stories can be quite fun to tell.

Much like a doctor who needs to determine the cause before he treats the symptom, so too do we need to get to the root cause of bad service before we can fix it.

In my experience, four causes of bad service continually rise to the top. There may be others, but these four are prominent, and in no particular order.

Low Expectations

The first cause of bad service is low expectations on the part of leadership.

Here is a strong statement: Show me a frontliner who is consistently rude to customers, and I'll show you a principal who doesn't give a rip about customer service.

It may sound harsh, but can anyone really disagree? Leaders who allow, or even demonstrate, poor service would be foolish to think this problem is just going to someday clear up on its own.

Changing a customer service culture is not a grass-roots effort. It is heavily top down. While top down sounds old school, and may not be a popular concept these days, the preparations for quality service have to start at the top. If friendly schools are the goal, then excellent service must be both demanded and modeled by the principal, superintendent, board members and other leaders. Set the expectations high and then hold everyone accountable to those expectations. A true leader will not demand staff to serve others with kindness without first doing so him/herself.

Also, do not waste your time aiming for perfect service. It's not realistic and only leads to frustration. Instead, aim for excellent service, and do not compromise. You will begin to see significant results.

Lack of Training

A second cause of bad service is training – or the lack thereof. Schools are notorious for hiring new staff members and putting them through an onboarding process that includes important topics such as how to fill out your tax forms, how to complete your mileage reimbursements, where to submit your vacation requests, and the like.

Rarely is there a point where someone directs us, "This is how we are going to treat people," or, "This is how we are going to make people feel." Instead, we are left to rely on our own instinct, on what we feel is right, based only upon service habits we picked up at a previous job.

We are kidding ourselves if we expect excellent service without comprehensive customer service training.

Rules

A third cause of bad service is rules. Sometimes our school or district may have rules in place that make excellent service improbable. An example of this is when I used to work in an office that conducted school district business with many parents on a daily basis. In fact, to handle the load there was a particular form that parents were required to fill out and submit. We had a rule that the form had to be submitted in person or by U.S. Mail. Electronic submissions and fax submissions were not allowed. Parents were understandably incensed by this outdated rule. I too could not understand why it was maintained as a standard operating procedure. At the time, I was told it was because we needed an original signature, however I think it was more a case of "we've always done it that way," which is a terrible answer.

Examine your rules periodically, seek out antiquated procedures, and try to look through the eyes of your customers. Ask your customers directly if there are rules that they see as nonsensical. You may be surprised at their answers.

Poor Hiring Decisions

Another cause of bad customer service is poor hiring. Hiring decisions are crucial to the health of any organization, but particularly a school system. It is difficult for a school district to dismiss an employee, especially for offering poor customer service. Unless they steal money or pinch someone, you may be stuck together for thirty years!

You may have heard it said that we should "hire the smile." Hiring the smile is a good approach because, while job skills are obviously important, skills can be learned. It's much harder to teach someone to be happy.

Also, consider the questions you ask in your interviews. Think about how you may want to screen these candidates. (I sure hope they smile in the interview!) Attitude, personality and integrity are difficult to teach. A new hire with the right kind of character has potential to become a great employee. Schools are a people business. Candidates who prefer working in a cubby all day and not interacting with people are probably better suited for a different line of work.

Chapter 8: What the Research Says

Some of you are statistic hounds, always sniffing around the research. In research there is a phenomenon labeled "confirmation bias." That is, we like to find research that backs up our beliefs about a certain topic. For instance, with confirmation bias, I suppose you and I, and a handful of our friends, could all examine the same set of statistics and come up with vastly different conclusions.

Having said that, I believe you will find the following statistics interesting. Indeed, the stats below may help paint a picture in your mind, and possibly even help you contemplate the potential reasons behind the numbers. Sharing these numbers with your co-workers could lead to a series of interesting conversations.

United States Department of Education Survey

Although it is a bit dated, I believe the numbers are just as valid today as they were when the research was conducted in the 2006-07 school year. It comes from the United States Department of Education and purports to measure the percentage of students in grades K through 12 whose parents reported being "very satisfied" with the way school staff members interact with parents. The numbers below represent those parents who reported they were very satisfied. In a perfect world, every parent would be very satisfied. That is our goal. Unfortunately, according to the research, we appear to be falling quite short in that area.

Size of School Breakdown

The first breakdown looked at the number of parents who were very satisfied with the way staff interacts based on the size of the school. They categorized the following: schools with less than 300 students, schools with between 300-599 students, between 600-999 students, and schools with 1,000 or more students.

As you may have guessed, the highest score was for schools with less than 300 students. In fact, 65% of the parents in those schools were very satisfied with staff interactions. Think about that for a moment. If 65% was the highest score, it means that *over 1/3 of the parents were not very satisfied*. Ouch!

As we move into the bigger schools, the score predictably drops. Schools with 300-599 students scored 58%, and 57% for the schools with 600-999 students. Schools with a thousand or more students bottomed out with only 45% of parents saying they were very satisfied.

Not trying to be too harsh, but all of those numbers are pitiful. Interestingly, and not in a good way, the range of satisfaction rates between the smallest schools and the largest schools was 20%. That's an enormous difference.

Questions need to be asked. Why would smaller schools be seen by parents as offering such better interactions? I'm sure we could all list a reason or two. I suggest we figure out what is working, and why, then apply those strategies to all of our schools.

Student's Grade Level

The next category was the student's grade level. The research indicated that 67% of parents whose students were in kindergarten through grade 2 reported being very satisfied with staff interactions. That number dropped to 63% for parents of students in grades 3-5. Then it dropped off a cliff to 51% in grades 6-8, and dropped again to 46% in grades 9-12.

So, we see a 21% drop from the start of the school experience to the end of the school experience. Questions arise as to what causes that drop.

Are middle and high school staff members really not interacting favorably with parents? Or have parent perceptions (or interactions) actually changed over the course of their child's school years? Again, great topics to discuss within your school or district.

Race and Ethnicity

The next category was race and ethnicity. Interestingly, parents of Hispanic students showed the highest rates of being very satisfied at 59%. Close behind were the parents of Caucasian students at 57%, followed by parents of Asian and Pacific Islander students at 50%. Parents of Black students measured at 49% and the parents of students who marked Other also measured at 49%.

The disparity in this category had the smallest range, only 10%, meaning there wasn't as big of a difference from one race to another. However, we cannot pretend there is no problem.

First, we need to drill down and uncover why there is any difference at all. Then we need to lift all the scores. Remember, the highest score - which was only 59% - was not even close to acceptable.

Parent's Education Level

Finally, the study looked at the education levels of the parents and how that impacted satisfaction rates. There was a correlation between the parent's education level and satisfaction with staff interactions.

The research shows that parents with higher levels of education actually are more satisfied with the staff interactions. Specifically, 62% of parents with graduate or professional degrees indicated they are very satisfied, followed by 57% of parents with bachelor's degrees, 53% of parents with vocational, technical or some college, and 51% of parents with a high school diploma or equivalent.

Hmmm...Do parents with higher levels of education somehow extract more satisfactory service from school staff? Perhaps they actually get more favorable responses to their requests, leading to higher satisfaction? Is that a form of favoritism? Is there such a thing as "gaming the system?"

Hopefully, none of those questions are indicative of what is actually happening; however, we cannot close our eyes to what the data says. It is our obligation to ensure that every parent, regardless of education level, race, size of school, age of child, or any other categorization, receives a level of interaction that would cause them to answer "very satisfied."

Chapter 9: Common Shortfalls

For years I held a narrow view of customer service problems, thinking they were specific to my school district. However, as I began working and visiting with schools and districts throughout my state and eventually coast-to-coast, I discovered that some customer service liabilities are universal. As we discuss them here, it may be helpful to determine whether these are areas in which you and/or your team struggle.

Inability to Reach a Live Person

The first common shortfall we see everywhere is the customer's inability to simply reach a live person. This one has been angering customers for generations, and is applicable to many industries, not just education. Now, more than ever, "live" people are less accessible. Many organizations make you push a series of buttons and endure a sophisticated automation experience before you eventually reach a live person. Face-to-face interactions are commonly replaced by sophisticated kiosks at grocery stores and airports.

Call me old-fashioned, but I like the reassuring tone of a good customer service agent, and I do not think I am alone in this preference. People need basic human interaction. Most of us would like a real person to assist if we have a question, offer a smile and wish us a good day.

Underused or Overused Technology

Following up on the first shortfall, there seems to be a lot of technology underutilization and overutilization, and we need to find the sweet spot somewhere in the middle. We should always be looking for more fresh, effective ways to serve our customers. If there is a device, an app, a web-based solution, a software option, or any technological tool that can make us better at what we do, then we need to be open to giving it a shot.

However, if we rely too much on technology and remove the human interaction, we will be getting away from the kind of service our customers really desire. You might want to take a look at your practices and see where you fall in the technology realm of customer service.

Inconsistent Information and Practices

Inconsistent information and practices are extremely problematic. Customers love to go answer shopping; you know, talking with everyone in your office until they get the desired answer. Consistency is key in these situations. One way to ensure consistency of information is to utilize an informational storehouse that can be easily updated, such as a website or an online electronic folder full of shareable documents. The storehouse needs to be both familiar to, and accessible by, anyone who will be assisting a customer.

As for consistency in practices, a standards manual would be a great start. Each customer service representative, whether staff or volunteer, should be issued a customer service standards manual that is packed with clear and measurable expectations.

Frontliner Is Not an Advocate

Another shortfall I notice occurs when the frontliner is not an advocate. What do your customers really want from you? They want you to be their agent, their representative, and their personal attorney going to bat for their cause. They want an advocate, someone who will not only point out a solution, but who will take them to that solution, and will co-own their issue. Too often, customer service reps put up a distinctive barrier that clearly signifies that the customer's problems are not our problems.

In reality, the best customer service agents will go beyond surface level interactions. The best customer service agents will share in their customer's sadness, despair and angst, but also will celebrate their customer's victories. Every customer should get the same level of service we would offer to a loved one. Consider the concept of advocating for your customers.

Lack of Return Messages

A common shortfall that can quickly tarnish a reputation is a lack of return messages. There is a simple solution for this one. When someone takes the time to leave you a message, return the favor. If a customer leaves you a voicemail, email, text, instant message, or especially, a hand-written note, simply return the message.

One frequent mistake is when a customer service representative avoids returning the message because he or she is trying to gather all the information in order to have a more productive conversation with the customer. While that may be well-intentioned, and sounds reasonable in theory, the problem is that gathering the information can take a while.

Without a return message, the customer doesn't know that you are gathering information, but may think you have forgotten, or simply disregarded the message. The fix for that is to return the customer's message as promptly as possible. You do not need to have all the necessary information. Simply tell the customer that you are working on tracking down the needed information. If the customer knows you are working on it, you can realistically expect a fair amount of grace. If the work on your end is taking considerable time, you can check in periodically with updates. Customers love being kept in the loop, even if an answer isn't available yet.

A Rushed Tone

The last common shortfall is the dreaded rushed tone: when the agent is trying to rush a customer off the phone or out of the office. My guess is that you have experienced this as a customer – and found the whole experience rather agitating. It's not fun.

Now, if you are a customer at a place that has a line of customers out the door, and is woefully short-staffed, you may understand why the representative wants to move the conversation along quickly. Surely, you would not want to be that customer who continues to chat with the rep just because you "waited in line and now it's my turn." You recognize there are others needing help and know the staff needs to keep things moving.

However, even if the agent is helpful, you are probably less likely to give the experience a positive grade if you feel you were moved along. To that end, be on the lookout for your own rushed tone.

As a reflective exercise, it might be worthwhile to look over these shortfalls and think of the one that you most want to guard against. It could be one that you struggle with personally. After you have made your selection (and this may be uncomfortable), tell a co-worker which one you selected and ask your colleague to watch for that behavior in you and to hold you accountable by letting you know if that behavior is detected. It may be hard to be confronted with that kind of truth, and it certainly requires a sizable dose of humility, but it will absolutely make you a more effective customer service representative.

Chapter 10: Tips for Good Service

There are a few undisputed tips for good customer service that you can integrate into your everyday service habits. If done successfully, you can reasonably expect happier customers and fewer headaches. Later in the book we will discuss more specific actions to take for good service, but these are a great start.

Know Your Customers

The first one is really simple: know your customer. Beyond just learning names, which is definitely important, learn what makes your customers tick – both individually and as a collective group. What are their expectations from the school? What are their preferred ways to communicate? Consider not only the content of the message they need from you, but also the venue, tone and timing.

Be on Time

It is imperative to be on time with your promises. Rounding off is not acceptable. If you promise to return the call by four o'clock, then stick to it. Half past four equals failure. Customers are usually willing to give us a chance to win their trust. It is a bad idea to waste that opportunity by being late on a promise. If, however, you realize that you are not going to be able to make your promised time, please contact your customer to let him or her know the new estimated time. Be sure to apologize for the delay and give an explanation if you think it is appropriate. This is not an ideal scenario, but far better than simply being late on your promise.

Along those same lines, if you can, *over* deliver when possible. That is to say, go beyond your promise and beyond the customer's expectation. If you promise to have it ready by four o'clock, and you have it by two o'clock, you will have earned both the favor and the trust of your customer. This is something to consider when you are making your original promise.

Consider Your Customer's First Impression

Consider the first impression being offered at your school or office. Try to see yourself as a customer — as a first-time visitor. Take it all in from the very beginning. Consider signage from the main road to the school. Think about directions to visitor parking and the main entrance. Is there litter? Is the paint peeling? How is the landscaping? These things make a big difference.

Sometimes the smallest things that would require very little to no financial investment could be the things that provide an excellent first impression. For example, have you ever thought about brightly colored vinyl banners welcoming your guests? They are inexpensive and easy to clean.

What do your customers experience once they come inside? Consider all the senses: the smells, the sounds, the sights.

There is a science to first impressions. We need to be cognizant of the customer experience. Survey your customers, or at least your first-time customers. Remember, first impressions apply to all modes of service, not just face-to-face. We also have to think about the first impressions we make when we answer the phone or send an electronic message.

Offer Options

Another tip for good service includes offering choices. Many organizations provide a menu of options when offering online service or as part of an automated phone system. We can also do the same with our walk-in customers. Everybody loves having a choice. They may not always be feasible, but when possible, choices can certainly enhance the customer experience.

Know Your Role (Stay in Your Lane)

Know your role. Even though no one likes to be reminded of this, it is nevertheless relevant. We are all customer service representatives – regardless of the title on our employee badge. We all have a responsibility for taking care of the customers. However, there may be some components of your customer service plan that fall primarily to you, and others that fall to someone else.

As an example, in some schools the principal may want to be the one to conduct all tours for new or potential students. That same principal may want all new student registrations to go through the data manager. There is nothing wrong with this plan as long as everyone is clear regarding their duties and as long as there is a backup plan for when the principal or data manager are out. Of course, the more we cross-train, the better we can meet the diverse needs of our many different customers. But for the sake of good service, there may be times when we simply need to stay in our professional lanes.

Be Accessapproachable

Accessapproachable. This made-up word describes a very real, very important concept. Back in the day, we used to emphasize the need for all customer service representatives to be *accessible*.

However, what we discovered was there are some folks out there who, although extremely accessible, are not so *approachable*.

Have you ever had a co-worker tell you, "Come by anytime, my door is always open?" The only problem is, after leaving their office you found yourself shaking your head and hoping you would not have to cross paths with that person again any time soon. That co-worker is certainly accessible, but not approachable.

Hence, the new word: accessapproachable. (Try dropping that into a dinner conversation this weekend!)

Chapter 11: Four Modes of Service

There is a pretty short list of ways we interact with our customers. Let's call these the four modes of service. I will explain what they are, and then we will spend the next few chapters diving deeper into each.

Face-To-Face Interaction

Face-to-face interaction is the mode of service that seems to make people the most nervous. However, if done correctly, this is also the most satisfying for the customer – and the most rewarding for the service provider.

The reason it is frightening is because of the pressure that accompanies this mode of service. There is no button to push that will put our customers on hold when they are standing right in front of us. We cannot disengage with them over the phone or simply postpone answering their question like in other modes of service. We have to come up with a way to meet their needs immediately.

The key is to be prepared for a multitude of various circumstances. The more we prepare, the easier it will be.

In a face-to-face encounter, we communicate in three distinct ways.

First, we have words. Words have the ability to be confusing or harmful when used carelessly, but comforting and informative when properly utilized. Choose your words carefully.

Of course, much of the impact of our words relies on the tone with which we speak. While words often represent what we want our customers to hear, tone relays what we are feeling. Tone adds emotion, and emotion tends to rule the day in the world of communications. Tone is like the behind-the-scenes look at what the speaker is really thinking.

Hopefully, we can apply a tone that matches our words and their intention. However, that should not always be assumed. Perhaps our parents were right when they instructed us to "watch your tone."

Finally, people see you, with their own eyes, in a face-to-face encounter. That means there is a physical component to your communication... I'm talking about body language, or gestures.

Just like your tone gives validity to your words, so your body language also conveys a story. In a perfect scenario, your body language sends your message. However, left unchecked, your body language can tell a counter story that creates doubt in your customer.

For example, we have all experienced a restaurant server who introduced herself by saying something to the effect of, "Hi, welcome to Jimmy's Diner. My name is Donna and I'll be taking care of you tonight."

While the words are ideal for the customer experience, and her tone was welcoming, Donna's posture and facial expressions clearly told a different story. She may have been looking around while introducing herself, checking her watch, or in some other way distracted. She didn't look you in the eye, nor was there even a hint of a smile.

No matter how appropriate or well-scripted the words, unfitting gestures can dilute, mitigate or even totally transform your communication... and not in a good way.

Keep in mind, gestures, tone and words are neither negative nor positive. They are simply tools at our disposal.

Just like a screwdriver is a great tool for household repairs, that same screwdriver can be a terrible weapon if used improperly.

Likewise, our gestures, tone and words can also be either constructive or destructive.

Phone Calls

Assuming you are not doing much video chatting as part of your service, you do not have the luxury of using body language with your phone customers. That means your words and tone are going to increase in importance. Research says our words *double in importance* from 7% of our communication in a face-to-face encounter to 14% in a phone conversation. But that's not the biggest increase – the tone you use jumps from 38% to 86% in importance when engaged on the phone.

Let us pause and process those numbers. When you are on the phone with a customer, 86% of what you communicate is conveyed through the tone of your voice. Along those lines, do you believe you can tell when the person on the other end of the phone is smiling? Of course you can, and that person can also tell if you are smiling. I don't claim to know the physiological reasoning behind the facial muscles that engage when smiling, or their impact on your tone of voice, I just know I can tell by your tone when you are smiling.

I encourage you to place a small mirror on your desk, and look at it while you are talking on the phone. If you look grumpy, then rest assured you sound grumpy too.

Test this theory for yourself!

Email and Social Media

The third and fourth modes of service are both electronic – email and social media. Many school folks are serving customers electronically, and rightfully so. This is a great way to communicate and meet needs. It can also be very efficient, especially when you consider some of the time-savers that accompany electronic customer service, such as the ability to respond to multiple customer questions at the same time, and being able to copy and paste responses as needed.

This mode of service has the least amount of pressure because the customer is neither standing in front of us breathing down our necks, nor getting antsy on the phone while we try to work out a viable solution. Electronic service grants us an opportunity to track down answers and proofread our responses, editing them as needed before sending.

But here's the catch…we do not have access to the tools mentioned earlier. We cannot use body language or tone in social media or email. Now, of course, we create a tone with our choice of words, but that is very different than the spoken tone we might use in a phone or face-to-face conversation.

Our communication when conducting electronic service is 100% based on the words we choose to use, and we have to be careful how that written tone may "sound" to our customer.

Chapter 12: Face-to-Face Interaction

There is a frequent question I hear in our training classes: "When multiple customers are seeking my attention at the same time using different communication modes, which one do I attend to first?"

That is an important question, and an issue with which we all wrestle.

The top priority is always the customer who made the most effort to get to you. In short, the walk-in customer always goes to greater lengths than the phone, email or social media customer, so that is who we serve first. Of course, you don't hang up on a phone customer if a walk-in shows up, but we'll address that shortly.

Suddenly they appear – live and in the flesh! Like mentioned previously this type of interaction can be the most anxiety-inducing, but that doesn't have to be the case. I have seven tips that I believe will make your face-to-face interactions both enjoyable and productive.

Greet Your Customer

First, greet your customer. I am often disappointed when conducting customer service audits at the amount of time it takes to be greeted...and sometimes I am not greeted at all!

I can count the number of staff members who walk through the office area, sometimes talking among themselves, but without greeting me. Perhaps they thought surely someone else had already greeted me.

How should we greet our customers? It's simple: with a smile! Here's a good rule of thumb for all in-person greetings, and phone greetings for that matter, smile before you speak! Don't say a word until you have smiled.

Acknowledge Your Customer

Next, acknowledge your customer. This is especially relevant when you are currently assisting another customer. We mentioned earlier that we should always serve the customer who made the most effort to reach you.

However, if you are already engaged on the phone, and another customer walks in, simply acknowledge your walk-in visitor. A simple "I'll be right with you" will suffice — as long as you smile while you say it. Make eye contact to let the customers know they have been seen. Nobody is going to expect or demand that you hang up on your phone customer. Always acknowledge, even if you are unable to help at the moment.

Stand

I am surprised in our live classes by how much pushback there is for this tip. That being said, for my staff, I expect us to stand as we greet our customers whenever possible. I do not like to have the customer standing over me, as happens when I sit at my desk. I want to be eye-to-eye when saying hello.

To illustrate, when you come to my home I do not sit on the couch and yell, "Come in." No, I stand and greet you at the door. Once inside, I invite you to sit, and when you sit, then I also sit. It should be no different at the office.

Another great benefit of standing along with your customer is you can somewhat control the duration of the visit. If a situation demands we spend significant time together, then certainly we both need to sit.

However, I like to determine the issue and find out what is going on while still standing. In many cases, I can answer the question quickly, or help the customer in some other way, and then proceed to closure. If seated, customers do tend to stick around longer. If your office functionality is dependent on getting them in and out efficiently, then standing is a great tool for you.

Just as an aside, please never tell your customers to "Have a seat" or "Take a seat." I know when I've been driving for any length of time, or perhaps sitting in traffic, I would rather stand for a while. I like to stand, stretch, and look at the stuff on the walls...and walk around a little bit. A better suggestion is to instead say, "Make yourself comfortable," or "Make yourself at home."

Use Your Customer's Name

Next, try to use your customer's name. Everybody loves to hear his or her name. The best way to learn their name is by telling them your name. "Hi, I'm Jeff. How can I help you?"

I like to offer a handshake if I sense it would be appropriate. Usually the customer will answer by giving their name, and then explaining the reason for the visit. Try to commit that name to memory and use it later in the conversation. You can make the name transaction a little easier by wearing a name badge and making sure there is a nameplate on your office door or on your desk that includes your name and title.

If you work in a school, you have the luxury of getting to know many of your customers by name. After all, you are likely to work with the same customer for years. Central office folks may have a little more difficulty in this area as you may only see a customer once or twice, so remembering names can be more difficult. However, it can be extremely effective in making them feel comfortable.

Provide Souvenirs

Give your customer a physical souvenir. The easiest and most professional way to do this is to simply hand them a business card. Every person on your staff, regardless of title or job description, should have a business card. They are inexpensive and some school districts even have their own print shops. I can order hundreds of cards for next to nothing. Having a business card with name, title and contact information raises the level of professionalism in any office. I love to finish my interaction with a walk-in customer by handing off my business card and inviting further dialog. "Hey, thanks for coming by. If you think of any more questions, don't hesitate to call on me." Customers will eat that up!

Another great souvenir is a simple brochure, or even a one-pager that contains basic facts about the school. I love for a front office person or an administrator to reach behind the desk and hand over an up-to-date brochure about the school that includes important information and also markets the school. These do not have to be professionally done. After all, it's not about the amount of gloss on the paper. However, they do need to contain accurate information, and under no circumstances can they contain a spelling, grammar, spacing or syntax error. Please proofread them carefully. They go a long way to upgrading the level of service, and are another inexpensive item to create.

Remove Physical Barriers

Consider the physical barriers in your office. Is there a desk, counter or window that would seem to be a barrier?

Some schools and offices are designed that way with safety in mind. I get the whole safety factor, and I am all for it, but we have to admit that sending these signals is very different than welcoming our parents as partners in the schooling process.

I have seen some barriers that require the customer to speak through a small window – like at an old-fashioned bank. Others have high counters like a newer bank. Either way, these are barriers that send a loud and clear message about your role versus your customer's role in the conversation.

It is understandable that changing the layout may not be an easy or cheap fix if you have a permanent physical barrier in your office. But perhaps you are in an office where the barriers are not permanently attached. Take a look at the arrangement of your furniture, and specifically your desk, to determine if a more inviting environment is possible.

In my school district's welcome center, we had two counters for serving customers. I decided that rather than standing behind the counter to greet my guests, I would move to the side of the counter and take a more casual pose. I wasn't invading their personal space – it wasn't an aggressive or intimidating move. It was simply an effort to remove the aura of the barrier and create a vibe that made customers, especially first-time visitors, feel welcome.

Always be on the lookout for ways to make our offices professional, but not rigid.

Escort Your Customers

Consider, when feasible, escorting your customer to the door once your conversation has concluded. I realize it is would be problematic to leave the office to escort every customer around campus. However, most offices are pretty small...only a few steps from the desk to the door.

Remember the old saying, "If you really want to know a man, walk a mile in his shoes?" Well, every customer wants you to be his or her personal advocate, the personal agent. Walking your customers to the door is a great way to bring closure to the conversation while simultaneously assuring them you will be happy to assist again in the future. This is where you shake hands if appropriate, give a business card and smile one last time.

These are suggestions for serving walk-in customers. It is not our expectation that everyone will employ every one of these strategies. However, take them out for a test drive! Not just once or twice, but put forth an honest effort before you stick them on a shelf. You might just see a difference in your customer response.

Chapter 13: Telephone

(Four-Part Greeting)

A few chapters back we discussed research that found all phone communication is the result of one of two components: words and tone. With the importance of words and tone, let us address the proper way to answer your phone. But first, a story.

In our live training classes, we like to hand out phone numbers for each participant to call. We do not tell them whom they are calling, just that it is another school or district in some other part of the country. We take a short break, and they go make their phone calls posing as prospective parents moving into the area and seeking information about the school. When we get back together, we ask them two questions: Whom did you call? Would you put your child there?

Interestingly, about half of the participants tell me they do not know whom they called. The representative on the other end of the phone either did not share that information, or rambled through it so quickly it was unintelligible. When I ask if they would put their own children in the school they called, the answer is frequently "No, not a chance." These are professional school people making the calls, and from one short phone call they have already made a judgment that their child is not going to attend that school. How much more emphatic would a parent be who is not a school person? We can talk about proper telephone protocols all day in a training session, but it doesn't get real until they actually make the live calls. That's when it all starts to come together. I guess you really have to experience it as the customer!

Smiling Buffer

Answering your phone should include the use of a four-part greeting. The first part is what I call the smiling buffer. This is the very first thing you say when you pick up the phone. Frankly, the words you use really are not overly important, as long as the tone is friendly. Chances are, your customer will not hear the beginning of your greeting. You can say, "Good afternoon," "Thank you for calling," or simply, "Hello." Just make it inviting and mind your tone.

Name and School/Department

For the next two parts of the four-part greeting mention your name, then your school or department. It does not matter which one is first, as long as you include both. Mentioning your name creates a bond with your caller and also adds a measure of built-in accountability. When the caller knows my name, I am naturally more apt to offer better service.

If you would like to have some fun, next time you call a business or organization, and the representative who answers the phone does not provide a name, ask the question, "With whom am I speaking?" There is often a short pause, then comes the response, "This is Susan." You can sense the agitation in her voice. Why should she be upset?

We can save the frustration for both the caller and ourselves by simply inserting our name into the greeting.

Offer to Serve

The final component of the four-part greeting is the offer to serve. The most common offer is simply, "How can I help you?"

I have to say the best four-part greeting I ever heard came from the least likely place, or so I thought. One morning I woke up and realized we had no hot water. The hot water heater had finally given out, so I found a phone number for the place to get it fixed. I am not certain why I expected the worst, but figured I would hear something like, "What up, this is Lou..." Instead, I heard this angelic voice with a perfect textbook four-part greeting that ended with the best offer to serve. She asked, "How can I make you smile today?" Wow...that was different!

After hearing it, of course I had to gather my staff together and explain what happened and how we should give that a try. They thought I was crazy (or more crazy than usual). But we gave it a test drive. What did we learn?

First, we learned there are some perverts among our customer base. Aside from that, the most common response was a brief period of silence, then usually an attempt at humor. The customer would try to think of a clever comment. It helped to diffuse our ornery customers as their tone shifted from anger to sarcasm. Handling sarcasm is much easier than handling rage!

So, if you want to use that offer to serve, "How can I make you smile today?" I would suggest you try it on a Friday afternoon before a long weekend, when you are actually in a really good mood and your tone is extra happy. Try taking fifteen or twenty phone calls that way and see how it goes...just for kicks. Otherwise, a very simple four-part greeting is a great way to set the tone for a productive and professional phone call.

Now, in full disclosure, I have had many people fight me on this. They say the four-part greeting takes too long and that the caller does not want to listen to all of that.

Well, let's see.

"Good morning. This is Jeff at Smith High School. How can I help you?"

Spoken clearly, it takes less than three seconds. But if I leave out any part of that greeting, and the customer has to ask me, "Who are you?" or "What school is this?" it can add ten seconds or more to the conversation. Taking care of it in a professional way at the front end of the call is actually a time saver.

Try writing out a professional four-part greeting, then answer your next twenty calls that way. Over the course of your twenty answers, this greeting will become your new habit. The four-part greeting is an easy-to-implement, professional upgrade to your telephone service.

Chapter 14: Telephone (Voicemail)

This chapter covers one of the most abused technologies used in school and district offices (and on cell phones) – voicemail.

Too often, it is not being used to its fullest capacity. Let us consider the twofold purpose of a voice mailbox. First, it is a way for me to leave a piece of information for my customer. It can be as simple as the fact that I am not at my phone, or, it could be more detailed, such as our new office hours, a change in the option menu, contact information for another person who can help, etc.

The second purpose is for my customer to leave a piece of information for me.

Following are a few tips for better utilizing your voicemail.

A Friendly Tone

Be sure your voicemail message has a friendly tone. Your caller may be disappointed not to reach you live, so at the very least, make sure your tone is welcoming and encourages the caller to leave a message for you. Many people do not like to talk to a machine, or will not leave a message for some other reason. Try to be as welcoming as you can and convince the caller you truly are interested in hearing the message and will respond upon your return.

Shorten Your Message

Most voicemail recordings take too long; eliminate the unnecessary. Try this exercise: Call your own phone number and write down your exact message, word for word. If you get tired of writing it, then guess what? We are tired of listening to it. It is too long!

Eradicate the nonessential words or phrases, such as "I'm not here right now," or "Leave me a message after the beep." Voicemail has been around long enough that we already know and understand how it works. Boil down all those words that are simply unnecessary. Whatever remains is your message. The shorter, the better. If your caller is still on the line and planning to leave you a message, then all he wants is to get to the beep. Get him to the beep as quickly as possible.

Real-Time vs. Generic Message

Decide if you will use a real-time message or a generic message. A real-time message is something that is updated frequently; every day at a minimum, maybe even more frequently than that. Your real-time message might sound something like, "Hello, you have reached the voicemail of Kelly. Today is Wednesday, June 4, and I will be returning calls after 2 p.m. Thanks." Beep. It is short, contains no unnecessary words, and gives the caller the most important piece of information – when to expect a response. Real-time messages are really great for the caller on the sole condition that they are *always up-to-date*. Your real-time message can never, ever be behind, or you will alienate your customer. After all, there's only one thing worse than getting a voicemail when you call, and that's getting an outdated voicemail that gives the impression it is never checked.

For those who choose to employ the real-time message, please avoid the play-by-play. No need to tell the caller everything on your agenda. Avoid wanting to provide your entire daily calendar. "Hello, today is Wednesday, June 4th and you have reached Frank's office. This morning I will be meeting with the mayor, followed by lunch with my agent. After that I will be accompanying my wife to her beauty pageant…" Nobody cares and nobody is impressed. Just tell me when I can expect a return call, and get me to the beep!

If you are the type of person who wakes up each morning and re-sets your voicemail recording without fail, then the real-time message could be very effective for you. However, if you are not that person, then you may prefer to roll with a generic message. "Hello, you've reached Sam's office. I look forward to talking with you very soon." Beep. This keeps it simple, and quick.

Mention the Names of Others Who May Receive Calls at Your Number

Finally, please remember to mention the names of everyone who may be receiving a call at your number. This is especially pertinent when you are taking calls for someone else or have your phone forwarded to someone else.

Consider this scenario: You may tell a caller you are forwarding him to Steve. Unfortunately, Steve stepped away and forwarded his phones to Tammy. Of course, Tammy is on the other line, so the call goes to her voicemail.

Keep in mind, you told the caller he needs to talk with Steve, and you were transferring him to Steve. To his dismay, the caller hears Tammy's message and assumes you sent him to the wrong person. Customers often refer to this as the "run around." It can escalate quickly into a more emotional situation.

It is all preventable.

* Note: Another preventable measure would be to simply not transfer the call to a voicemail without the caller's permission. In this case, I would stay on the line with the caller and let him know Steve is unavailable, offering the option to leave a message, call back, or give me a name and number so I can have Steve return the call.

Chapter 15: Email

Whether we like it or not, email is a very important part of our overall customer service environment. Most of us spend much more time working on email than we would like. Also, we have all been burned by an email message we sent out that was misinterpreted by the reader. As you recall from a previous chapter, email is not like phone or face-to-face service, as it doesn't have an auditory tone or visual gestures. The only tool we have is our words. They do convey a tone, but not one that can be heard – only one that is created in the mind of the recipient. Unfortunately, sometimes the tone received is not the same tone we intended as the sender.

Accurate and Appropriate

The information you send and the words you choose, in every email, without fail, should be both accurate and appropriate. The accurate part is easy. Everyone understands the notion of sending out information that is up-to-date. The bigger mistake in many email messages is the appropriateness. For instance, if you receive a simple email question like, "What time does your building open?" you could respond simply, "8 a.m." That might be accurate, but would certainly not be appropriate. The next few steps will provide the outline for an appropriate response.

An appropriate response would be something like the following:

> *Good morning, Mr. Davis, and thank you for writing. Our building opens at 8 a.m.*
>
> *Please call or write if I can serve you in any other way.*
>
> *Sincerely...*

Customer's Name

If you know your customer's name, always use it in your greeting. Unfortunately, sometimes the customer does not offer a name in the original message. In that case, obviously, you cannot use a name. Do not be fooled by thinking you can guess the name based on the email address. Just because the original message was sent by Valerie.Smith@whatever.com does not mean your customer is necessarily named Valerie Smith. It could be one of Valerie's family members, or just a made-up name. However, if your customer signs off the message with a name, then you can use that name to begin your response.

All of this, however, poses another dilemma – should you use the customer's first name, or should you begin with a more formal title such as Dr., Mr. or Ms.? There is not a one-size-fits-all answer, but I try to use first names as much as possible in order to create a more casual, friendly relationship. I want the customer to feel comfortable coming back to me with further questions or needs. After all, I make it a point to sign off with my first name as well. If, however, I perceive our conversation to be a sensitive, contentious or litigious matter, then I certainly want to keep my response formal.

Thank the Customer

Try to begin the body of the note by immediately thanking the customer for writing. It is a nice touch and sets a tone for what is hopefully mutual appreciation.

Friendly Tone

As previously mentioned, your overall email message does create a tone of sorts. Make sure yours is friendly. This is especially important when writing a message that might be somewhat delicate.

A good practice is to write your message, then get some distance from it for a few minutes. Run to the restroom, get a drink of water or just work on something else. When you return, read it again. You will likely end up changing something – and not because it is inaccurate. More frequently it is because upon re-reading it, you see how the tone could possibly be misconstrued.

Another great practice is to have a couple co-workers read your message prior to sending it. Ask them if they interpret it as off-putting or needlessly controversial. A fresh set of eyes can be invaluable. I do this frequently. By doing so, I encourage my co-workers to do likewise. It is a great habit for the entire team.

Forwarding Messages

Many email messages that come to your office may contain questions that need to be answered by someone else, perhaps an expert from another department. A good strategy is to forward the message to the expert, but also be sure to contact the sender and let her know that you have read the concern, and that you have forwarded it to someone qualified to assist.

Have you experienced this debacle? You diligently check your email inbox, read a question, and forward it to someone who can better address it. However, that person, for whatever reason, does not respond. Days go by and still no response. The original sender thinks you are ignoring them, but the truth is you responded right away. Ugh!

That problem goes away if you simply let the sender know that you have forwarded the question to the expert. Your customer will surely appreciate the correspondence, and may even thank you for taking the question seriously and directing them to a solution.

You may go one step further by also letting the sender know the name and email address of the person to whom you forwarded the message. That way, the sender can follow up directly with the expert if needed.

Offer to Serve

When wrapping up the note, try to invite further dialog. This could be something as simple as, "Please contact me should you have any more questions."

Recall how we encourage every employee to have business cards and give them out to our walk-in customers? This is the same concept. We want our customers to know that we are here to serve them, and they should be comfortable asking.

Contact Information

Be certain your message has all of your contact information. Your auto-signature should include your name, title, school or department, address, cell phone, office phone, fax, and, yes, your email address.

Many seem to believe that since the message is being sent via email that the email address does not need to be included in the auto-signature. However, your customer may have a need to copy and paste your contact information, so be sure to include your email address in with the rest of the contact information.

A good rule of thumb is to contain in your auto-signature all the same information you have on your business card.

Proofread

Please, please, please proofread your message before sending. If necessary, have a colleague or two also proof it for you. If you worked in a different industry, perhaps there might be forgiveness for spelling and grammar and syntax errors. However, as a public-school employee, parents and community members expect – and demand – error-free messages. Fortunately, that is entirely possible as long as we take the time to proofread before sending.

Save Messages

It is good practice to save all of your email messages. Hopefully, your system archives them automatically. Be certain you can retrieve any message, those received and those you sent. You never want to get summoned to a meeting based upon an email conversation, and be the only person at the table without a copy of an email that you sent six months ago.

Newspaper Test

Make certain every email message you send passes the "newspaper" test. In other words, if your message was confiscated by a reporter as part of a public records request (and every message you send or receive is indeed "on the record"), would it be problematic if it was published in the local media? Think carefully about what you put in writing.

Some have argued that these components of an "accurate and appropriate" message require too much time and effort to include in every email we send. To that end, one strategy I would recommend is changing your auto-signature to encompass the components mentioned above. It could look something like what is written below.

Dear _____,

Hello and thank you for writing. _____

_____

_____

_____.

Please call or write if I can serve you in any other way.

Sincerely,

Jeff

[full name]

[title]

[school/department]

[address]

[phone]

[fax if relevant]

[email]

With this strategy, all you will need to do is write is the customer's name and the answer to the question. The rest will already be included in your auto-signature. It is easy, quick, professional, and, if done right, it ensures the opening and closing of your message will be error-free.

Check your own auto-signature and consider how you can use it as a tool to help upgrade the professional look of your email responses.

Chapter 16: Social Media

This chapter is focused on social media as a customer service tool. Though it has been around a long time, it is the youngest of our four modes of service, and the most fluid. It continues to morph as new communication tools are designed and start to catch on. Due to its agile nature, along with its frequently updated technologies, it is quite probable that some schools and districts may not be implementing social media to its fullest advantage. We find great variations in how social media is utilized from district to district, and even from school to school within a district. Having said that, there are still a few strategies we can put in place to help us use social media as a way to serve our parents and our communities.

Determine Purpose

Before you engage in any kind of social media on behalf of your school or department, it is important to determine your purpose. Are you hoping to market your schools? Change the culture? Build a reputation? Do you want to provide important information? Or are you simply trying to offer accessibility?

Lay out your purpose, or more likely, your purposes. Put them in priority order. Your primary purpose may change after a season, and that's fine. But to start, determine your purpose. That purpose will guide the rest of the decisions you need to make regarding the use of social media as a customer service tool.

Two-Way Street

Every social media tool, by design, is a two-way street. It is great for sharing news, but also for gathering feedback. If all you are doing is sending information, but not receiving it, then your social media is not much more than a trendier version of your website. To harness the power of the tool, be sure to implement variety in your social media communications. Tell stories, deliver announcements, and include pictures. Any communication you send that includes pictures or videos typically gets a stronger reaction.

The same is true for your email messages, presentation slides, birthday party invitations or any other communication. Pictures continue to be extremely powerful. Using video can get even more powerful results.

* One hint for video...shorter is better!

Identify Your Tone

Next, identify your tone. Some school districts have gotten cute in this area, literally. One of the nation's largest school districts recently earned a national reputation for their *sassiness*. That was a conscious decision on their part, and it was done in a way that the community really enjoyed. I don't think I could pull off sassy very well, so I have avoided that in my school district. How about you? Have you decided on a social media tone? Maybe your tone is serious, playful, clever, thought-provoking, academic, or practical. Reflect on this notion, and consider the pros and cons of each tone before settling in where you are comfortable AND can be successful. Be careful not to select a tone that will set you up for failure.

Plan for Responding to Questions

Sending messages and posting information is easy, but what is your plan for questions or feedback from your customers? You will need to be ready, because the finer the job you are doing in the social media realm, the more interaction you can expect. Have a plan.

Beware of Over-Dependency

Along those lines, watch out for over-dependency. Social media can become addictive; it subtly consumes more and more of your time and resources. Before you know it, you are neglecting other customer service tools because you are entirely wrapped up in social media. That's not healthy. Remember, it is only one of many tools in your customer service tool belt.

Professional Language

Professional use requires professional language. It is tempting to slide into an overly casual verbiage. Many of us have personal accounts that occupy much of our time away from work, and we may have a certain vernacular that is acceptable there, but not necessarily in our professional accounts. This holds true for shortcuts, abbreviations, emojis and acronyms. Be cognizant of your language and your customer's expectation, particularly as you work in an education setting.

Avoid Being Defensive

When using social media, avoid being defensive. There are many customers in "Cyberland" who will not hesitate to take shots at school staff members any chance they get. They may take your story or announcement and somehow mangle it up and use it against you. They may call you out in front of all your other online contacts, or they may openly criticize you or your colleagues by name. Though despicable, it happens. Be careful that you do not slide into a defensive position. There is so much you might like to say, but there is so much more you may regret. Avoid allowing some cyber punk to lure you into a messy situation.

Over-Promoting

Some organizations use social media to engage us, but then we quickly find out it is a bait-and-switch tactic. We were hoping for expressive dialog, new information and important announcements, but all we got was repeated commercial advertising. It does not take long to disengage and disconnect.

Make certain your school and district social media conversations are more than self-promotions. Sure, some of that is appropriate. Perhaps we should do more of it! After all, our parents and community members want to hear about all of the great things going on in our classrooms. Share the awards, the victories, the "attaboys." Invite your community to celebrate along with you. However, also use your social media accounts to engage in honest dialog – get the community involved in problem solving. Gather input needed for big decisions. It is all right there at your fingertips.

Regret

Never post anything on your social media accounts, professional or personal, that you might regret. If you are unsure, it is probably wise to refrain. Even if you take down a post, it can be archived and used against you.

Remember the newspaper test from our email chapter? Well, the same applies to what you post on social media. Keep in mind, your personal accounts are not immune to public scrutiny.

A hokey reminder: If you think you might regret, keep it off the Internet! Feel free to share that one. Or, how about this: If in doubt, don't send it out!

Know Your Boundaries

Know your own limitations in speaking for your school or district. Also know your specific role. When you start engaging electronically, it is very easy to overstep your jurisdiction. You may know an answer to a question, but it may not be appropriate for you to respond. There are some answers that need to come from a school principal or a departmental leader. If that is you, then have at it, or if the leader has deputized you to provide that kind of detail, then go for it. But, if not, be careful not to overstep.

Always Professional

Before you engage in your social media strategy, please re-read through these tips. If you put these into play, you will indeed appear professional to your customers. Professionalism should be your chief strategy and measuring stick. If you always stay professional, social media can be a delightful tool for you, and a wonderful gift for your supportive community.

Chapter 17: Multicultural Service

Our next chapter centers on multicultural customer service. There are some excellent tips for those times when you find yourself in a situation where cultural or language barriers may factor into your ability to serve.

Billy Joel, the famous musician, was once quoted as saying, "No matter what culture we're from, everyone loves music." Now, you will surely find varying styles of music prevalent in different cultures, but music is a universal concept that is an important part of every culture. Along the same lines, there are differing ways of interacting with dissimilar cultures, but there are some universal truths that will overcome any mistakes.

Never Fear

The biggest mistake I notice is fear. Many of us freeze with uncertainty when trying to help customers from other cultures. We lack confidence and are afraid of offending. We mean well, and we genuinely want to be helpful, but in our fear, we are actually doing more damage than if we tried and failed.

How should we approach customer service with our friends from other cultures? The answer is not nearly as hard as you may think.

Start all conversations as you would with friends from the same culture. Simply acknowledge and welcome everyone. The same rules apply. Begin every transaction with a smile, and be friendly. They will know that you intend to help them, and that immediately gives you the benefit of the doubt as you progress with your conversation.

Open-Ended Questions

Throughout your conversation, be sure to ask open-ended questions rather than yes/no questions. Yes/no questions, or questions that allow for single word answers, may not get to the heart of the need. It is too easy for a customer to give up on an area of need by simply answering yes or no or picking an answer from a list of choices you provide. This is especially true when a language gap exists. Even if it takes longer and requires more effort, questions that force a more detailed response will get you to the real issue at hand so you are able to provide the needed assistance.

Prepare Ahead of Time

One great idea is to prepare ahead of time. As best you can, get to know your audience in order to avoid offensive behaviors. For example, if you serve a large population of Norwegians, it would be worth your while to study up on the country of Norway and its people, their customs and especially their gestures, to make sure you don't accidentally offend anyone. To that end, be sure to use your tone and gestures when you do not have the possibility for words. When the language just isn't working, your tone can still convey a message, as can your gestures. Just be sure your gestures aren't offensive. How will you know? Prepare... and study the cultures of your customers.

Effort Matters

Keep in mind, effort matters. The fact that you are trying your best will resonate with your customers. They know it is difficult. Imagine the challenges they face on a daily basis! They know it is not going to be easy, but the fact that you are giving it a solid effort will mean more to them than you might realize.

Enjoy Diversity

It is very important that we learn and appreciate diverse cultures. Look at diversity as a wonderful addition to your school or district and not as a separator of people. Your learning environment will be enriched as a result. Have fun learning about other cultures. Make friends with your customers, and let them know how much you appreciate the opportunity to learn more about their customs and traditions.

Start with a Smile

Please start and end every interaction with a smile – and smile throughout your conversation. Like Billy Joel and the music, the smile is also universal. Every culture smiles. Your customers will greatly appreciate it, and it will make your interactions more pleasant.

Chapter 18: Delivering Bad News

One area of customer service that requires a higher level of skill – some might even call it an art form – is the ability to deliver bad news.

If you have been in this business for any length of time, you know that a big part of your job is giving parents, students, and even staff, answers they do not want to hear. We spend a good amount of our time telling people 'no'. If you have ever had to deliver it, you know the discomfort that comes with delivering bad news. It's never easy or fun.

There is no magic formula for making bad news sound great. However, there are a few strategies we can implement that might make it go a little better, or, more likely, a little less bad.

Deliver in Person

If possible, deliver bad news face-to-face. This can be much less comfortable, and can be intimidating, but the person receiving the bad news will usually appreciate your effort – maybe not immediately in the heat of what might be an emotional moment, but later, after the dust settles, they will appreciate it.

Think back on the chapter regarding face-to-face customer interactions. In person, we have the ability to use tone and gestures in addition to our words, and tone and gestures communicate more than words. Delivering bad news face-to-face provides you with those helpful tools.

Prepare Your Tone

It is always useful to prepare your tone prior to the conversation. Practice it. Decide how you want it to sound. There can be a fine line between sounding authoritative versus sounding like a bully. If you are communicating bad news in writing, please have a colleague read it over before you send it out – not so much for the message, or even the clarity, but for the intonation. Ask your proofreader how this message makes him or her feel. Then make the needed edits before actually sending it out to your customer.

"No, but…"

One helpful strategy is to replace a flat 'no' with a more helpful "No, but…" If a parent asks you, for instance, to call a teacher down to the office for a conversation, instead of saying 'no' you might try saying, "No, *but* I will be happy to share your number with the teacher so she can call you when she isn't with students."

Keep in mind, when we say 'no' to a customer without any alternative offer, we are simply drawing a line in the sand, daring our customer to cross it. The customer is likely to see that as the school official winning…and the customer losing. That may get us the desired outcome on some occasions, but it can also be unnecessarily explosive.

Think back to the earlier chapter on *Customer Needs*. One of those primary needs is for the customer to always *retain dignity*. Offering another option is one way of meeting in the middle, removing the "I win, you lose" feeling that may come with just 'no'.

It may not always be possible, but when you can, try to use "No, but…" You will likely find a calmer and more understanding customer.

Stand on Policy

When you have to deny a request, try to stand on policy or some other written explanation. This helps you in multiple ways. First, it removes you as the object of your customer's scorn. When you can show them the rule in writing, your role quickly morphs into merely the messenger. The messenger is a good spot when you find yourself in those situations. Your customer may still be angry, but that anger will be directed at the policy, and not at you.

In fact, if you share that written explanation with kindness and tact, you may actually win the favor of your customer and find yourself in a place where you can actually be of assistance, rather than having to defend some rule or policy that you did not create. You may even be viewed as a knowledgeable resource.

Additionally, from the customer's perspective, it helps to have a policy explained and visually shown. It lets the customer know that the denial of his request is not specific to him, and not done on a whim. Rather, the denial of the request is in adherence to an established guideline that is consistently applied to all such requests. It is fairly administered.

Having a written policy or rule also makes it more believable. You have probably experienced a situation in which you delivered bad news to a customer and the customer did not believe you, or wanted to know where the policy was located on the website so he could see it for himself. When something is in writing, it carries authority.

I personally experienced this phenomenon a few years ago when I found myself struggling with a school board policy. It was very unpopular among our customers, and seemed to be the basis of far too many emotional conversations. Customers did not believe me when I explained the policy, and they frequently wanted to debate the uselessness of it.

One day I took a few minutes to type up the policy and encase it in a plastic display on the front counter of the welcome center. I was floored by how much easier my job was when the customers could read the policy for themselves. I was no longer their enemy.

I guess the old saying is true, seeing is indeed believing. The same policy...written instead of spoken. What a difference!

Take the High Road

No matter what the customer says to you or about you, keep in mind *you* are the professional. Do not be lured into an argument. Do not get defensive. Simply maintain your composure and never forget that the customer, while venting at you, is not upset with you in a personal way. You just happened to be the lucky employee who had to deliver the unwanted answer.

Remember, the customer is really upset about not getting whatever it was that he or she wanted. The customer is upset at getting denied or declined. Do not take the insults personally, and please do not take that frustration home with you. Your family and friends deserve better.

Days later, when this issue has come and gone, you can take comfort in knowing that you kept it professional – that you stayed on the high road.

Avoid Appeasing with False Hope

Sometimes the temptation exists to tell customers what they want to hear simply to avoid controversy and, frankly, to get them off your back. Please do not appease with false hope. Do not sugar coat the possibilities just for the sake of ease. Be honest, even when that means delivering the exact news your customer does not want to hear.

Consider this: If you think your customers are going to be upset upon receiving the bad news, imagine how much more they will lose their minds when someone else in the organization has already told the customer a hopeful outcome to their request, and then you have to tell them it has been denied.

We need to take our medicine and share the bad news right up front. Never mislead your customer with false hope. Remember to stand on the policy or written explanation. You will be glad you did.

Future Interactions

Your delivery of bad news may not necessarily be met with open arms. However, never let an outcome impact future interaction. Whatever happens, if anything negative is said, or if the customer storms out of the school mad at you and the entire school district, or even if the customer insists on talking to your boss or to the school board, the reality is you may have to work with that customer again in the future. If it is a parent, then you may have to work with that customer for years to come. Avoid carrying forward any negativity into future interactions.

Additionally, avoid letting a difficult conversation with one customer seep into interactions with other customers. Every new conversation is a new opportunity.

Chapter 19: Difficult Customers

Difficult customers come in all shapes and sizes. They bring varying types of problems, different types of needs, and share one commonality — interacting with these folks is probably the most stressful part of our jobs. I think this is why our difficult customer section is always one of the most popular components of our live training sessions. We like to sit around with others who are in the same line of work and swap stories about the crazy people we encounter. You probably have the best stories at the dinner party simply due to the level of crazy you face on any given day!

The good news is there are strategies you can implement to make your interactions with difficult customers a little more tolerable.

In our live training sessions, we like to put the class in groups and assign each group a fictional difficult customer. One group may get Willie Whiner, another Whacked Out Wendy, Haughty Henry, Vanessa Victim, Political Polly or Outraged Oscar. We give each group a brief description of their difficult customer, and then have the group create a list of strategies to use when dealing with their specific customer. It's amusing to have the group share their list with the class and then have the class add strategies of their own.

Interesting side note: One time I was training a group whose assigned character was named Pompous Paul, and a member of the group informed us she knew exactly how to handle him – because he was her ex-husband!

What we quickly discover is that the savvy customer service rep needs to have many tools at the ready for these occasions. For instance, we have talked a lot about tone throughout this book. When helping Belligerent Bryant, a soft tone is probably best because it brings the conversation to a place where we can get past the accusations and emotions – actually working together on a solution. However, when Basket Case Barb comes strolling in with her cornucopia of problems, claiming, "Nobody can ever help me," and "I never can get the right answers," and "Please don't pass me along to someone else," she needs to hear a very confident tone. The decibel level may rise slightly with Barb. She needs to know that her problem will be met head-on and that she will not be left to fend for herself.

Tone is just one example. There are many across-the-board strategies you can implement when working with difficult customers. Below, are a few strategies I highly recommend.

Listen

Simply listen to your customer. It is easy to hear your customer, but it takes some effort to truly listen to their specific needs. If you find yourself in a face-to-face interaction, perhaps you can make notes as he or she describes the issue. If you are engaged in a phone conversation, perhaps ask the caller to slow down or even repeat something to demonstrate you are paying close attention. All customers, just like all people, want to be heard.

Affirm

You do not have to agree with what your customer is saying. In fact, in many cases you probably will not agree. However, you can affirm your customer's sense of dismay by using phrases like, "I can see why that would be a problem," or "I understand why that would be frustrating."

Be Honest

Refrain from telling your difficult customer something untrue simply as a sedative. As mentioned in our chapter on delivering bad news, you can expect that tactic to return to haunt you. Though not the desired answer, even a ranting fool will appreciate a truthful response. It may be later, after a cooling off period, but they will greatly prefer honesty over pacifying falsities.

Keep an Open Mind

It can be especially tough when entertaining the same difficult customer over and over again, but keep an open mind.

"Oh, here comes Grumpy Gilbert, wonder what he's complaining about today." But what if Gilbert, just this time, is justified in his complaint? Maybe this is the one time he is right.

As the customer service representative, it is easy to think we have seen and heard it all. Sometimes we may find ourselves answering a customer's question before they finish asking it. But you cannot know for sure until you hear them out...same with Old Gilbert. No matter how much of a thorn in your side he has been over the years, because he is your customer, he deserves the benefit of the doubt. Keep an open mind and resist the strong temptation to apply past experiences to a current interaction.

Stay in the Now

Resist getting caught up in conversations that use words like "always" or "never."

"This school always confuses its parents." "I can never find the information." Forget about all of that — stay in the now and focus on the current issue.

Perhaps you can bring the conversation back on topic by saying something like, "What brought you in today?" Or, "How can I help with the situation that led you to call us?" If there are ongoing, or lingering problems, you absolutely should address those, but first you need to take care of the issue at hand.

Compete Mode

This is a tough one. If you are like me, there are certain words, phrases or even gestures that light my fire. They send me into compete mode. If you have ever experienced that, then be sure to keep watch for whatever triggers that response in you. Sometimes the transition from serving your customer to competing against your customer can be subtle. You may find yourself long into a deep discussion and not even realize that you are debating rather than assisting.

Not to belabor the matter, but what is it we hope to accomplish by "winning" a conversation? By beating our opponent...er...I mean customer? There is no prize – unless ego inflation has value (I would argue it only brings trouble). There is nothing to gain from squashing your customer like a bug, even one that may have been particularly annoying. Be on your guard not to fall into compete mode.

Emotion v. Logic

You may have heard it said that "emotion eats logic for breakfast." I believe that to be true. Emotions guide us all...no matter how much we try to suppress them. That is just how we are wired. In fact, a good rule of thumb for all of us would be to continually strike that ideal balance of emotion and logic in our own lives. Too much of one and not enough of the other will cause unwanted problems.

A great many of your most complicated customers are probably dwelling in the realm of emotion. And why not? They are coming to you because they feel that something has happened to them or to their child. They may be upset because Junior got suspended. Perhaps Sally didn't make the cheerleading squad. Whatever it is, no matter how petty it may seem to the rest of us, their issues strike an emotional chord within them, and now they are bringing those issues to your office.

The fact that you represent an institution like a school or district probably serves to heighten their emotions, not quell them. It is likely that by the time they get to you, they are pretty amped up about their problems, and you will need to walk a fine line in order to avoid making matters worse.

There is not much assistance you can offer while they are emotional, but if you can help them transition into the realm of logic, there might be an opportunity to provide genuine help.

So, the big question is this: How can you move your customer out of the realm of emotion and into the realm of logic? The best way to make this transition is through the use of questions.

Questions

Using questions is another great customer service tool. In our live training sessions, I always like to ask my classes, "When you get a ranting customer, how long do you let that customer go on before you interject?"

Some believe the customer should not be allowed to rant at all. Others may let the customer go on indefinitely. Many try to quantify by suggesting a time limit – such as 30 seconds, or perhaps two minutes.

For me, the most effective strategy is to let customers continue with their rants *until I hear them repeat themselves*. Once they repeat themselves, I know they have shared all the information they possess that could potentially be helpful when we begin working toward a solution.

They may have a detailed list of fifteen reasons why I should be fired today because one of my school buses backed over their mailbox (you think I'm making this up!), and I'll let them go through everything they want to say, but only until I hear the same thing again. Then I know they are done.

This is where questions become relevant. Once they have indicated an empty tank, jump in with a question.

"Mrs. Jones, did you say this happened around 4 o'clock yesterday?"

"Yep, I sure did."

"Mrs. Jones, did you also say those were yellow paint chips you found by your broken mailbox?"

"Yes, that is correct."

"Mrs. Jones, did you mention that you saw what appeared to be school bus tire tracks in your yard?"

"Yes..."

See what is happening here? I am slowly but strategically hijacking this conversation, and I am relying on questions to make that happen. I also employ another effective customer service tool: tone.

Each time I ask Mrs. Jones a question, what does she do? She answers it, because it is related to her story. It shows I was listening. Then I ask another question. She answers again. Then another question. She continues to answer. Each time, I soften my tone a little bit more. It does not take very long until I am driving the train. Once I am driving, we talk about facts and use our inside voices. We have entered the realm of logic.

The use of questions, along with a soft, but purposeful tone, allows us to transition from the realm of emotion to the realm of logic. It is there we can actually work on a solution for our customer.

Chapter 20: Handling Criticism

Unfortunately, criticism comes with the territory when we sign up to be public servants. In fact, the people we try to serve are the very ones bringing the criticism...ain't that a kick in the shorts?!?

I have a few thoughts about criticism, and how to handle it when it comes your way (notice I did not say "if it comes your way"). Allow me to share.

Strike the Balance

On one end of the spectrum is the potential to be crushed by criticism. If you are not careful, you can let it change you in ways that are unhealthy for you, and unproductive for your work.

If the criticism is of your work, then you must not take it personally. However, if the criticism is of you – or your character – then it is clearly a personal issue. Either way, you must keep it in perspective. You cannot let it hinder the service you provide to children and families on a daily basis.

On the other end of the spectrum lies the potential to completely dismiss the criticism – to not give it a second thought. This is not healthy either. It is actually good to reflect on what is being said. There may be something in there that is useful, something that will make you a better service provider – or maybe even a better person.

Strike that balance between being completely crushed and completely dismissive.

Consider the Source

Next, we must take into account from whom the criticism is being dispensed. Receiving criticism from a co-worker who is widely known throughout the community as a gatekeeper, and considered rude by parents, is very different than receiving criticism from a trusted mentor who has invested countless hours into your personal or professional growth.

Before we make major changes to our service habits, we also need to consider the intention of our critic. Does the critic truly mean to be helpful (even if the words feel harsh)? Is the critic merely advocating for a child? If so, can we really be upset about that? Is the critic interested in a win-win solution? Is the critic looking out for the best interest of the school/district/community?

Before we can properly strike that aforementioned balance between being crushed and being dismissive, it is a good idea to give careful consideration to the source of our criticism. The source will surely be a determining factor in how we react.

Avoid: Being Defensive, Blaming Others, Excuses

When criticism arrives, whether in person, in an email, via social media, in a note, on the phone or spray-painted graffiti-style, one natural tendency for many of us is to lash out with a response that ultimately comes off as sounding defensive, blames someone else, or offers an excuse for our shortcomings.

I believe all of us have instinctively utilized these three techniques at one time or another...and probably with regrettable results. These are not endearing reactions, nor do they lead us to a workable solution. They make us look petty, guilty and clueless...like we simply don't get it. Be careful not to let this become your reputation.

Respond/React Later

Regarding the three negative techniques mentioned above, none of us want to be defensive, none of us want to pass the blame onto others, and none of us want to issue excuses.

These are not the strategies we deploy when we have had time to think about our criticism. Instead, these are instantaneous responses. To that end, we are better off not reacting to criticism right away.

Our off-the-cuff responses are more likely to be bad decisions. Instead, give the criticism time to soak in. Consider the source, the intentions, and the potential outcomes...then react. You will be glad you waited.

Look for Nuggets of Usefulness

One thing we have not mentioned yet is the content of the criticism. If we can examine what was said, aside from any emotion that may be evoked, and simply examine the core message, maybe, just maybe, there is something of value in there.

Even if we have little or no respect for the critic, or, if we are angered by the way the criticism was delivered, we would still be wise to examine what was said. Someone took the time to make this criticism known.

If there is just one thing I can learn from it – whether it is a change I need to make, a mannerism I need to adjust, new information about a different culture, or even affirmation of something I am doing well – it is worth a deeper dive.

Try to take something away from every experience.

Be Humble Enough to Admit Mistakes

My final strategy for handling criticism is perhaps the hardest of all – genuine humility.

Criticism, as painful as it may be, can be life changing. It can be a great teacher, a great motivator, and a great accountability partner...but only if we are humble enough to accept it.

We may believe the criticism is unfair. We may think the critic is spiteful. We may feel stabbed in the back or publicly emasculated. However, at the end of the day we must humble ourselves to the point where we can honestly ask: Was the criticism warranted? Was I in the wrong?

If so, be humble enough to admit your mistakes. After all, criticism should be seen as an opportunity to grow. We would be foolish to expect growth if we cannot first admit our mistake, and then seek out solutions for improvement.

Chapter 21: Crises Communications

It is often said the crises build character. Maybe, maybe not.

Someone much wiser than me once told me that crises REVEAL character. This I believe whole-heartedly.

Having been through many crises at both the school and district levels, I can unabashedly say that our character will be unveiled, for better or for worse, in a crisis.

Along with our character, another decisive factor in determining whether we successfully contend with a crisis is our ability to communicate in crunch time. If you spend your career working in a school or district office, you can expect many emergencies – and you can also expect to have a critical role in communicating with administration, staff, parents, students and local authorities.

If you find yourself in a crisis, the following tips will help you communicate in a way that is effective – bringing stability, understanding and reliability to a situation that could quickly turn disastrous if mishandled.

Prepare

It is difficult – some might argue impossible – to prepare for every detail of every potential crisis. However, the more you are prepared, the better your chances for making the right decisions when calamity arrives.

Be sure you are familiar with all the up-to-date crisis information, and you know how to quickly access it just in case you need it during the storm. Because we are talking about communication, know how to use all the tools. Know, or know how to access, the needed user names and passwords. Have a plan for reaching your hard-to-reach families. Stay in close contact with those who can translate messages into the languages spoken in your community. Know how to reach the various community agencies and authorities.

Also, always know your organizational chain of command. When a crisis hits, you should have no questions about what is, and is not, your role. Clearly defined roles will make a huge difference.

Follow Orders – Nobody Goes Rogue

I once had horrific crisis in one of my elementary schools in which we received a report of an active shooter on campus. The news helicopter was flying above the school before we could hang up the phone. It was a day like no other for me.

The good news is, there was no shooter. However, one of the problems we faced regarding communication in the heat of the moment was from a school employee with good intentions.

Of course, the school was on full lockdown. Students and teachers remained in their classrooms and silent while police swept the building. One teacher, in an effort to calm the parents of her students, used her cell phone to send messages to her parents letting them know her class had been cleared and all students were safe.

While that sounds very humanitarian, she strayed from the emergency plan. Many parents have more than one student at that school. When they receive a message from one child's teacher, but not the other child's teacher, that can cause panic, hysteria, and irrational behavior – and create a very dangerous situation.

It is crucial that everyone knows and adheres to the emergency plan. Nobody goes rogue!

Consistent Messaging

Consistent messaging is important all the time, but even more so in a crisis.

Despite who is speaking, the message should be the same. You cannot have the principal telling parents one thing, a front office member telling staff something different, and a superintendent telling the press something else.

Be sure the message has been fact-checked, it is relevant to the issue at hand, and appropriately delivered. Be especially careful that the English version of your message is consistent with any translated versions. Everyone in your community deserves clean information.

Tone – Not Too Big, Not Too Little

When you are communicating in the midst of a crisis, keep in mind what was discussed earlier in this book regarding tone. It is a powerful tool. It can cut through barriers, bring meaning to a message and cause the recipient of the message to comprehend and remember it.

However, used inappropriately, tone can be offensive, can rob the messenger of relevance, and can provoke undesired emotional outcomes.

In crisis communications, you are probably not using your messages to persuade, but more likely to inform. Along those lines, monitor your tone to ensure you are not making the problem bigger, but also not making light of the crisis.

There is an old saying regarding the press...its job is to report the news, not create the news. Do not let your tone make you part of the story. Let your tone convey that you are calm, you are composed and you are here to help.

Timeliness – Frequency, Relevance, Order

One thing we have learned about communicating in a crisis is that frequent communication is extremely important. Even if there is nothing new to report, we still send out a message letting people know the current status and that we will be back in touch very soon.

Remember, you are inside the crisis. You see it through a very different lens, you have a task, and maybe even some level of control of your environment. However, those with whom you are communicating are feeling completely helpless. They want to help, but there is nothing they can do – except wait. They are counting the seconds until they get that next update.

Be sure your communication is relevant. Don't play games. Don't be cute. Your communication needs to make sense. While on the topic of relevance, also consider the methods you will use to collect information in a crisis.

It is also important to consider the order of your communications. By that I mean who you contact first.

Of course, the urgency of the crisis may dictate the order of communication to some degree. However, I learned the hard way that there are many messages that need to be sent to members of the school board, or perhaps to principals, **before** they get distributed to the general public. Sometimes that means sending the same communication multiple times, inserting a set amount of time between each send.

I find this a frustrating task. Part of me wants to say this is causing us to work harder, not smarter. However, at the end of the day, the board members, principals and others are likely to get bombarded with questions, so giving them a preview of the message before it goes public is greatly appreciated.

Accuracy – No Speculating, No Opinions

I cannot find the words to caution you strongly enough to avoid guessing and avoid opinions when communicating in a crisis (actually in all communications, but especially in a crisis).

On paper, it sounds like a no brainer. Of course, we will avoid speculating and throwing around our own opinions. However, when a crisis hits, and you are communicating, it is very possible you are going to get asked for more information, a peek behind the curtain. People want more than you can give them. In the absence of facts and clean information, they will gladly listen to anything you want to tell them. They may try to pressure you to give your thoughts on the matter, your estimate on when this will be over, your best guess on what caused it, etc.

Do not give in. Hold the line. Just like in a court of law, you speak the truth and nothing but the truth.

Closure

Finally, when your crisis has subsided, spend ample time reflecting on what happened. Determine what worked, and what you would do differently next time. Be sure your debriefing includes the communication efforts. I suspect your team will learn something new – likely many somethings – from each crisis. Be humble enough to take a very honest look and help one another assess the decisions that were made. This will help you be better prepared for the next crisis.

Chapter 22: Promise Statement

A few years ago, I was traveling through Maryland with my family, and we stopped at a Fairfield Inn. As I stood at the registration desk signing in for the evening, I noticed an interesting plaque mounted to the wall next to my head. It was clear to me that someone placed it in that particular spot strategically and intentionally to be noticed by visitors like me.

It was a promise statement written for the customers – and it was fantastic. It had a simple elegance that I found to be very effective.

This document contained three distinct sections. First, it had an opening paragraph that spoke about the importance of the hotel's customers, and how customer satisfaction was the priority. It was not fancy or flowery.

Next, it had a list of measurable promises. The list was concise and easily digestible. It included a small handful of items, maybe three or four, that they wanted to promise to their customers. The key was, those promises were easy to measure. Nobody would have to guess as to whether they were being kept – it would be evident to all.

Lastly, a closing paragraph invited the customer to hold the team accountable for their promises.

The bottom of the document signed off with something to the effect of, "Sincerely, Your Fairfield Team."

What I found especially interesting was that all around the margins of the document were actual hand-written signatures. Getting the corporate big shots to sign this before they sent it to all their hotels was a very nice touch...or so I thought.

I asked the hotel clerk about the document, and especially the corporate autographs. He was excited to tell me that those were not the names of honchos from the corporate office. Instead, one of the signatures was from the guy who cleans the pool. Another was a housekeeper. This amazing document was crafted entirely by the team at this particular hotel – a classy gesture indeed. What a surprising and fortunate turn of events. How much do you suppose this document cost them? Nothing. What a simple stroke of brilliance!

I couldn't wait to get back to the office and tell my team.

We gathered for a staff meeting and began the exercise. Coming up with the opening and closing segments was reasonably easy. The tricky part was deciding on a few solid promises to which we, both as a team and as individuals, were willing to be held accountable.

By the end of our meeting we came up with about 25 potential promises...far too many. We agreed to let that list percolate for a week. When we met one week later, we trimmed it down to four items.

This exercise produced great fruit for us in that it forced us to really peel the onion until we reached the core of our customer service existence. We had to prioritize, and then put it out there in a very vulnerable way.

We learned a few things along the way that may be helpful for your team if you should (and you should) take on this exercise.

Opening Paragraph

At the top of your document, paste in the district or school logo. This is how you know stuff is about to get real!

Then add a title that says in big, bold letters, something like, "Our Promise to You."

Next, write your introductory paragraph. Here's an example of a great opener: "Caring for our guests is a priority of this school. In fact, you are so valuable that each member of our team has made you a promise, signed it and displayed it for all to see as a reminder of your importance and our commitment."

Word it any way you like, as long as it is simple and easy to understand.

List of Measurable Promises

Promises are those specific services you pledge to fulfill for your customers, and upon which you want to be evaluated.
In my district we decided on five promises. You may want more or less than that, but I would caution against listing too many.

Here are the promises we chose:

- *We promise to always make you feel welcome.*
- *Always respond promptly to any need you might have.*
- *Always work to help you find solutions.*

- *Always be approachable.*
- *Always serve you cheerfully.*

Invitation to Hold Us Accountable

Your statement should conclude with your invitation to be held accountable. I would suggest something to the effect of, "If, for any reason, you believe we have broken our promise, please remind us immediately. After all, a promise is a promise!"

That's it. An effective promise statement does not need to be very sophisticated. It does not need to contain any Ivy League words – just a simple promise from your team to your customers.

It has been my experience that the customers love it, and my team was truly motivated to honor those written promises.

As they say, "What gets measured gets done." Well, once you put it in writing, get everyone to sign it, and put it on display for the world to see, you have no choice but to live up to it.

If you elect to create a promise statement for your school or department, try to make it a local exercise. It could be something done by your entire school staff, or maybe even just your office staff. Either way, it becomes more powerful when your team owns it.

Once you have decided on your promise statement, you can also add it to your website, print it on the back of your business cards or any number of other places. Publicizing it is important: the more visible, the greater the accountability.

Chapter 23: First Impressions

It is a good idea to note and understand the first impressions your school or organization creates. A great first impression, whether in person, on the phone, in an email or on social media, will cause you to have happier customers who just might be a little more willing to give the school the benefit of the doubt when things go awry.

In order to cast a discerning eye on a first impression of any type, you have to think like a customer, which is why you are probably the worst person to gauge the first impression being offered by you, your school, or your department. You are likely too familiar with it.

Someone else, whom you trust to share an honest assessment, ought to judge your school's first impression. If you can get inside the mind of your guests, perhaps you can see if there are some easy upgrades needed.

Another great way to do that is to visit other nearby schools simply for the purpose of checking out their first impressions.

Below are a few components the friendly school should consider.

Signage and Directions

Is your building easy to find from the main roads? Does your website offer clear and easy-to-digest directions? Can anyone answering your phone provide directions to a lost driver? Once in the parking lot, is it clear to the first-timer where to park and where to enter? These are all things to consider from the perspective of a guest.

Curb Appeal

When is the last time you really thought about your curb appeal? Things to consider include litter, rusted poles and doors needing to be painted, and landscaping that looks like it hasn't been addressed in decades. The thing is, none of those are big-ticket items. All can be done for little or no cost by district maintenance folks, a PTA workday, or students seeking volunteer hours.

Organize Your Lobby and Office

It is a good idea to make sure your lobby and your office have an organized look. When possible, utilize cabinets with doors rather than open shelves. Remove as much clutter as possible. Try to toss out anything that is no longer needed. You want your customer to walk in and think to himself, "These folks have their act together."

Waiting Area

In addition to looking organized, make sure your lobby and office also have a comfortable feel. Take a good look at your waiting area, the furniture and even the reading materials. When you are in your doctor's waiting area, you are probably looking around at brochures and flyers and anything mounted to the wall.

Think now about your office. Do your customers see trophies and awards? Photos of students and staff through the years? Historical information? Think of what you would like your guests to know and make sure it is easily available.

Have Your Mission Statement Visible

Be sure to have your district or school mission statement visible. It gives off the impression of a place that has direction and is focused on accomplishing good things for kids.

Smile

Smile before words are spoken. Whether you are greeting a visitor in person, or answering a call, just smile before you speak. It changes the entire customer experience.

Chapter 24: Reputation

Whether we have just met our customer for the first time or have been working with the same person over a number of years, we can use our customer service to build a positive reputation.

If you believe that, then the question is this: What is your school's customer service reputation?

Customer Service and Customer Retention

Business research tells us that acquiring new customers can cost a business five times more than simply satisfying and retaining current customers. That should resonate. I know it is a business statistic, but the concept of *retaining* customers being much easier than *recruiting* customers should be applicable to your daily customer service work.

Here is another statistic: A 2% increase in customer retention has the same effect on profits as cutting costs by 10%.

To put that in school terms, have you lost students in recent years to other options? Perhaps parents have pulled their children out of your school and enrolled somewhere else, or maybe they decided to homeschool. In any case, we have to wonder if some of those students were lost due to customer service issues, or perhaps customer service was just one part in a series of deciding factors.

Either way, when a student walks out that door, so does a significant amount of funding. It does not take many withdrawals until we are left trying to figure out what (or who!) we have to cut from our budget to make up for the loss of revenue. No school wants to see enrollment drop.

Here is one more statistic: The average business loses 10% of its customers each year.

What might those parents who left our school say about our customer service?

All of this talk about losing students is quite depressing. So, let's flip the conversation. What if we actually used customer service to recruit students instead of driving them away? What if we developed such a great customer service reputation that our service gets discussed at the soccer games, in the grocery store lines, at work, etc.? What if it became so great that people actually came purposely seeking out our schools?

We can indeed use customer service to build a positive reputation.

Customer service is about relationships. When you have a great relationship, you get the benefit of the doubt when an issue does arise. A great reputation for excellent service can help us overcome the occasional slip-up. Nobody is perfect, so why not build in a measure of forgiveness from those we aim to serve?

Here is one final business statistic: The customer profitability rate tends to increase over the life of a retained customer.

Imagine a new grocery store opens in your community. You go there the first time to pick up a few items, probably some of the more generic things like a gallon of milk and a loaf of bread, but really you just want check out the new store. You have a good experience and determine it is a quality store. You notice the deli section has a nice variety, so next time you go you add lunchmeat and a few more items to your basket. Before long you are going there with your entire grocery list. It becomes your go-to store.

You began by spending small amounts there but now you realize you are spending hundreds of dollars per month. Because the store was able to retain you as a customer, their profitability rate increased. They probably spent more money on advertising to draw you in as a customer, but keeping you didn't cost nearly as much. It is good business practice for them to prioritize your satisfaction and to keep you as a customer rather than to lose you and be forced to spend exponentially more money to advertise for your replacement. How much better if you, as an existing customer, tell all your friends about this fantastic store. The reputation will bring the revenue.

Our great service leads to an excellent reputation, which leads to success by any measure – higher student and staff retention rates, increased funding, and ultimately, happier customers.

Chapter 25: Selling Your Schools

Every member of an organization – whether a business, club, team, church, non-profit, government agency or anything else – should always be prepared to deliver a concise description of that organization, one that clearly promotes its value.

Remember the term "elevator speech" we mentioned in Chapter 2? If you are ever in an elevator with a couple of perspective parents who know nothing about your school, you have about fifteen seconds to wow them. What is the most important thing about your school? What is it you want them to know? You should have your answer ready at all times. You may need to break it out when you are standing in line at the bank, pumping gas, or meeting with your church group.

There are really three questions you need to answer in order to come up with a great mini commercial about your school.

What Is Your Goal?

To start, determine your goal. In fact, you may have varying pitches for different goals. You may have one pitch simply to recruit parents and students to your school. You may have a different pitch for getting a bond referendum passed at the polls. You may have another pitch for winning back the support of your community after a public relations disaster.

As an example, suppose your goal is recruiting parents and students to your school. Maybe you have a considerable number of students going to private schools, charter schools or being homeschooled. Maybe you have lost significant funding and even positions because these students, who live in your area, are not attending your school. Your goal in this scenario is to get families to choose you.

What Do You Want Them to Believe?

The second part is determining what you want your audience to believe about your school. What matters is that you have an answer. Never be caught off guard by this question...and never think you can simply wing it.

Before you decide on what your answer is, you will want to consider the needs of your target population. For instance, let us say you have a school on one side of town with a high per capita income. Most of its families have two professional working parents who take impressive vacations and have grand houses.

The school across town has a completely different demographic. It has a significantly higher percentage of students on free and reduced lunch, and many more single moms working multiple jobs trying to make ends meet.

What do you want these parents to believe about your school? If you tell the high-income parents that you are a nurturing place with a caring staff, the pitch will fail to accomplish your goal of recruiting parents and students. Why? This specific population does not seek nurturing – their children get that at home. They want rigor. They want to know that your school has state-of-the-art resources and world-class instruction. They want to be sure their children will be well-prepared for their arrival at the Ivy League school of their choice.

However, while our other school with the higher percentage of single parents certainly deserves rigor and great resources, that is second to their need to be assured that their student will be loved and cared for in a safe learning environment. If they are not able to spend as much quality time with their children, then they need to know that there are good, solid, trustworthy people at school who are going to look out for their kids when they cannot. These families may be more dependent on before or after school programs, and they need reassurance that the staff will protect their children.

Neither of these elevator speeches is better than the other...they are simply different – each tailored to the needs of a specific target audience.

In fact, within a single school you may have a variety of pitches for different sub-populations...multiple pitches for the same goal. Think hard about your goal and what you want your customer to believe about your school.

What Can You Deliver?

Once you have determined your goal and identified what you want your audience to believe about your school, then the last step is to make sure you can deliver on what you are promising in your sales pitch.

For example, if you determine that your community needs to hear a pitch about how your school is high tech, but in reality, your staff fears technology or uses technology as an over-priced babysitter, then you are unlikely to deliver on your pitch.

If what you can deliver does not match what you want them to believe, then you have two choices: change what you want them to believe or, better yet, build your capacity to deliver it!

This is a very important, often overlooked aspect of our work. No matter your title, the sales skill is part of your job.

Chapter 26: When Reporters Call

If we do a great job marketing our schools, then we should expect to receive positive attention. From time to time that attention may come in the form of a local reporter.

Unfortunately, you can also get a reporter's attention when you do not want it, like when a negative story emerges...or, as they say, blood in the water.

Nevertheless, whether you are being interviewed or simply welcoming a reporter while he or she is waiting in your office, you should always be prepared with actual strategies for interacting with the press.

Give Your Team Notification

The most important thing to remember about working with the media is this: Never speak with a reporter without first discussing it with the person in charge of the building or department. Always secure formal approval prior to conducting an interview.

In fact, many school districts, and organizations of all types, have strict protocols on who can and cannot speak with the media. These are in place for good reason.

Additionally, many school districts have a public information officer. That person may hold a title like director of communications, public relations, or similar. In addition to securing the permission of your principal or supervisor, also be sure to consult your public information officer before agreeing to the interview.

Having served many years as a public information officer in multiple school districts, I do not want to see a story on the news or in a newspaper that quotes one of my employees without my prior knowledge, and I *really* don't want my superintendent or a board member to ask me about something they may have seen in the media regarding our school district and for me to be caught off guard.

Keep this in mind...five-year-olds love surprises. Public information officers do not!

For the remainder of this chapter, let's assume you have contacted your public information officer and your supervisor to let them know a reporter is coming, and everyone is in agreement you should participate in the interview. Now you are expected to answer questions and provide comments.

Experience is a great teacher, and she has taught me many tough lessons, some the hard way, that I would like to share with you.

Reporters Are Not Your Enemy

Although it may occasionally seem like it, reporters are not your enemy. They are simply doing a job, just like you. They are trying to get a story to their editor or publisher that is timely, relevant and accurate.

They probably already have some of the facts before they arrive or call you, but may be digging for more. Other times, they may have most of the information they need for the story and simply need someone from the school to comment. Do not be that someone unless you have been designated as the spokesperson.

161

As a rule of thumb, you want the expert on the topic to be the one speaking. For instance, if there was an issue with a school bus, then the transportation director would be a suitable interview. If the issue is related to finances or budgets, then the chief financial officer might be appropriate. If something happens at a specific school, often the principal would be the most likely candidate.

As mentioned previously, your district's public information officer is well-suited to handle media issues, and needs to be given the opportunity, as well as all the necessary background information, to direct the process.

Reporters Can Be Your Allies

If treated with respect, reporters can be tremendous allies. Building strong relationships with reporters is always a good idea. Try to give them a quote or an interview whenever feasible to help them with their stories. Help them track down information as needed. Your efforts can pay fantastic dividends in a variety of ways.

Sometimes, if there is an event or a story that you would really like to see published, you may be able to call a few of your favorite reporters on short notice and provide the scoop. If you have developed enough trust, they might pitch it to their bosses so they could come cover it.

Other times, they might call because they received a tip from a parent and want to find out what is really happening. You might be able to tell them your version of the story, and even downplay the situation.

I have found that they will often give me the benefit of the doubt if I have proven myself trustworthy. As with all other aspects of customer service, relationships trump everything else...even with reporters!

It takes time and effort, but the dividends of a mutually respectful relationship are well worth it.

Nothing Is Off the Record

When reporters come to your school, or call you on the phone, or send you an email, you must remember there is no such thing as off-the-record comments. Do not say anything that you would not want your boss, or your loved ones, to read.

Be Poised and Professional

When the interview begins, always be polite, poised and professional. Try not to be hurried or short, nervous or fidgety. Watch your tone as you would with any customer. If it helps, ask a colleague to stand off to the side while you conduct the interview. There is nothing to be nervous about, though some get rattled by a reporter taking notes or by the camera, microphone and bright lights that are often used.

Try to stay cool and speak with confidence, and definitely try not to look like you have something to hide.

Your Message Is What Matters

This may surprise you, but the reporter's questions are really irrelevant — all that matters is what you say, so be sure to have a clear and accurate message prepared. Jot down two or three points that you want to emphasize and practice saying them prior to the reporter's arrival. Then, no matter what you get asked, you simply state your points. Resist getting baited into a different conversation.

Consider this - when the reporter returns to the station to edit the video or draft the story, all that will matter is what you said in the interview. Your words make up the complete set of material that will be available for the published story. The reporter is unlikely to include his own questions, but will be forced to decide which of your comments to use. If you provide great comments, you should be happy with the final product.

Beware of the Repeated Question

Beware of reporters who keep asking the same question. They may tweak it slightly, but they keep asking it looking for you to give a different answer. You have two choices here.

First, if the question is repeated, so is your answer. You can continue providing the same response.

Second, you can simply let the reporter know you have already answered that question, then ask if there are any other questions.

It Is Okay to Respond Again

Do not be surprised if you find yourself dissatisfied with a response you provided in your interview.

It is okay to ask the reporter, "May I try that again?" It has been my experience that the reporter will always grant you the opportunity. Doing so provides the reporter with a couple answers from which to choose when it is time for editing. If you give a more full or eloquent response on the second try, that "do over" may make its way into the final cut. That works in your favor.

Answer Concisely

When responding remember that time is important. Be concise. If you give long and detailed responses to a reporter's question, the reporter might only use a few seconds of that quote. You would do well to talk in clear, organized sound bites, whether you are speaking to a television reporter, a newspaper reporter, a radio reporter or any other type of press.

You want to provide something quotable, but concise.

Ask Questions of Your Own

The reporter is not the only one who gets to ask questions. Feel free to ask questions of your own. Perhaps ask about the story with questions such as:

> "Who else have you spoken with?"
> "How did you hear of this story?"
> "What other interviews are you lining up?"

Do not expect a reporter reveal sources for a negative story. However, if you have invested in a relationship, a reporter may tell you more than you would otherwise expect. By asking a few simple questions, you might be able to glean the reporter's angle, and that may prove helpful in formulating your comments.

"No Comment" Is Indeed a Comment

Please avoid saying, "No comment." Perhaps say instead, "I don't know, but I can try to find out for you." A reporter will probably not use that quote. However, if you say, "No comment," you can almost guarantee a reporter will include that – and that answer never looks good in print or on television

When Things Go Well, Shut it Down

Finally, every reporter likes to finish the interview by asking you, "Is there anything else you would like to add?"

Assuming you made your pre-planned points during the interview, the answer is a resounding "No." Once finished, it is a good idea to begin the process of removing your microphone and walking out of the camera view. Once you have accomplished your mission, shut it down.

Working with reporters should be the easiest part of your day. Enjoy the experience!

Chapter 27: Revival

Most of the tips, examples and theories we have discussed so far in this book are designed for *individual* improvements – mindsets and strategies you might personally implement to improve your own customer service delivery.

This chapter, however, is a little different in that it addresses strategies for elevating the whole team, the whole school or even the entire school district. This involves changing the customer service culture. We like to call it a customer service revival.

Identify a Customer Service Champion

For this revival to be successful, it is crucial that someone – the RIGHT someone – be tabbed as the leader. The leader has to want this role. It cannot be dumped on anyone. The leader should be respected in both title and character. There will likely be pushback on the part of some employees, so the leader must remain focused on the mission and not easily discouraged.

Cast a Vision

Like any attempt to change culture, it is helpful to start by casting a vision. Be sure your leadership buys into it whole-heartedly. If not, you will have problems right out of the gate.

Once you are certain that leadership sees the same vision, then you can begin the process of sharing that vision with your entire team. It should include everyone, top to bottom, in the organization. They may not all buy into it at first, and some may doubt it is possible, but it more easily leads to the next step, which involves setting expectations.

Create a Customer Service Standards Manual

One way to set clear expectations would be to create a customer service standard manual. This should be a document that clearly lays out all the how-to's, such as the expectations for signage and directions, the way we answer the phone, how calls are transferred, and directions for how soon we reply to email questions, just to name a few.

It should also point out the never-dos, like eating lunch at our desk in view of our customers or using text language in our email messages, and many other issues.

The manual is likely to be rather dry, and probably boring to read. It will be stuck on a shelf somewhere. But you know who really loves the standards manual? The most important people in our school districts: principals. Yes, I said it!

Having the standards in writing means we can now hold people accountable. It is difficult for a leader to say to an employee, "I don't like the way you treat our guests," or "I need you to interact better with other people." Those are generic and objective measurements, and invite much bigger problems.

For example, employees who think they are doing a nice job may feel picked on or singled out for reasons other than customer service. This can lead to discrimination cases and headaches for leaders. However, if you have a written standard manual, a principal or other leader can talk with an employee about a specific customer service expectation that needs improvement. A detailed manual provides a clear agreed-upon standard that makes performance evaluations more productive and less confrontational.

Make Your Customer Promise Public

A previous chapter discussed the *Customer Promise*, but it is also a good idea as part of a customer service revival. It sets up accountability to our parents and community members. Once you create one, make it public and let your constituencies know about it.

Train Continuously

Try to find ways for the whole organization to become trained. Also, once someone has gone through training, avoid checking it off the list as done. Training should be ongoing. Always be on the lookout for the latest and greatest strategies and technologies that can help you (and your colleagues) raise your game. Be sure any training you roll out promotes a customer service mindset AND offers practical tips that can be immediately implemented.

The idea is for all participants to take away something that will change the way they work for the rest of their respective careers – either a new theoretical approach to service, or a new habit that will be appreciated by customers.

Your training should have a healthy combination of theory and practice.

District Leadership Must Model Excellence

The very best service in the entire school district should take place in the superintendent's office. Likewise, the principal should provide the very best service at a school. Leadership has to model excellence. If not, then they cannot demand it from their people. Merely chatting up your staff about customer service revival or sending people to training is not going to work if the top dogs are not living by the same rules.

Measure Your Customer Service Performance

I have mentioned the phrase, "What gets measured gets done."

A customer service audit is a big undertaking and can be fairly expensive, but what a wonderful way to gather information and to quantify the customer service performance at every site in the school district.

You can also measure performance through surveys, customer feedback cards and focus groups. Be creative.

Adding a customer service component to every employee's year-end evaluation can also be a great way to increase the level of customer service accountability. This simple step makes it real.

I also suggest including a customer service component in the onboarding process for all new hires, and writing it into job descriptions. These are solid measurement strategies.

Recognize Those Who Do It Well

A great way to start changing the customer service culture is to publicly recognize those who are doing it well. You can easily brainstorm a long list of ways to accomplish that goal. For example, some of the school districts for which I have conducted customer service audits decided to use them as part of a reward program.

Instead of using the results in a way that is punitive or degrading, they used the results as a competition. The schools with the highest scores might earn a banner or trophy or some other desirable reward that they would be proud to display.

Staff members love to compete, and they love to be recognized for their success. Presenting those awards in a principals' meeting or a board meeting, and sending out a press release announcing your winning schools, are fun ways to earn recognition.

Find ways to recognize those who are making the effort to be customer service superstars.

Epilogue – Good Versus Great Service

We can learn great lessons from tragic events. In fact, I suppose it is rather tragic that it often takes a serious wake-up call to get our attention.

I received such a wake-up call some years back.

Early one morning when Lori and I were getting ready for work, the morning news was covering a story about a local police officer who had been shot in the line of duty. It was a routine traffic stop in the middle of the night. I imagine it started out similar to countless others he had initiated in the past. But this time, the person in the car shot him – right between the eyes.

We were stunned. You see, this officer was a neighbor of ours. More than that, his wife was my little girl's teacher. As you can imagine, he would periodically swing by the school and visit the classroom. The kids loved him. He was a real-life hero. Surely you can envision a playground full of kindergartners wanting to play and climb all over this very tall, very energetic police officer. He was so good for the kids.

So, how do I tell my six-year-old that her hero was shot, and is lying in the hospital fighting for his life?

I took the kids to school that day, and I can remember how eerily quiet it was in the hallways. This is a school known for its excitement and enthusiasm. But that day was distressing, tense and uneasy. Clearly the staff was aware, and they were doing their best to make school a normal experience for the kids.

While this event occurred in the middle of the week, I want to fast forward to the ensuing weekend. I was out in my yard, sneezing, coughing and wishing I could afford a landscaper, when it occurred to me that perhaps I should drive over to my neighbor's yard (the officer and teacher) and see if their grass needed mowing.

To be totally honest and transparent with you, and this is very embarrassing, I was really hoping their yard did not need any of my time. What I really wanted was just to feel good about myself that I went and checked. The mere fact that I loaded up my lawn mower and drove over there was rather righteous of me – even if I didn't cut any grass. That is messed up...I know!

Well, I arrived at their house and, sure enough, it needed mowing. The whole aura of being in their yard was kind of creepy. I felt like I was in a scary movie. Both cars were in the driveway, and I noticed all the signs of typical family life, the grill, the swing set, etc., except nobody was home. In fact, the heavy yellow pollen (North Carolina!) all over the cars told me they hadn't been moved in days. The family was apparently living at the hospital.

I fired up the lawn mower and got started. Interestingly, after about ten minutes, I began to experience this peculiar sensation. I was overcome by a genuine sense of humility – clearly a virtue that was lacking in my life. I didn't immediately recognize what I was experiencing.

After twenty minutes, I was walking around the yard behind my lawn mower with a stupid grin on my face. Somehow, I felt really good. I wanted to do more for my friend, perhaps clean his gutters, trim his hedges, or maybe fix something. However, I know my limitations. I'll never be confused for a handyman.

But what was that sensation? I learned a lesson that day about servanthood. I actually humbled myself, and took on an unpleasant task for the sake of someone else without any payment, award, attaboy or even a thank you. In fact, to this day, the family never knew I cut their grass one Saturday years ago, but I remember it vividly. It was a life lesson that was long overdue.

For once in my life, I set aside my own plans for the benefit of someone else. I sacrificed whatever time, energy and resources I had available in order to help out my neighbor – and it felt really good!

I look back at that event, and years later I can clearly see how it relates to customer service. This hard lesson is undeniably applicable to distinguishing between **good** and **great** service.

You see, *good service is all about what you do*. If you do the things mentioned in this book, you will be good at customer service. I believe that I offer good service based on the things I do when interacting with my customers.

However, great customer service is an entirely different ballgame. *Great service is all about who you are.* It flows from the character you possess, the integrity rooted deep within you. Great service rises up from this foundation when you are serving others.

Great customer service requires the same humility I learned about when I was cutting my neighbor's grass.

Granted, there have been times when I have indeed been great at customer service...times when I have set aside my pride, and humbly served with that same level of submission and sacrifice – expending my time, energy, knowledge, and any other resource I could muster – all for the sake of a customer.

And let me tell you, providing great customer service is extremely rewarding. But it would be untruthful for me to lead you to believe I treat all my customers that way every time. I want to, but the reality is I don't. It is my goal, and I know I have a long way to go.

Perhaps you live on that mountaintop of great service. Maybe you give all you have for the sake of your customers in every encounter. If so, I applaud you and hope that you are enjoying the satisfaction and good feelings that come with that kind of humility.

Currently, I only have a time-share on that mountain, but I hope to one day join you as a permanent resident. It is a beautiful place filled with beautiful people.

If the service you are currently offering is not good, then I encourage you to implement the many strategies included in this book. Doing those things will make you good at customer service.

However, if you are already doing those things and you are offering good service, then I challenge you to push yourself to great service. Examine your character, your humility, and your consistency. It's easy to offer great service once in a while, or to offer great service to friendly customers. The hard part is offering great service when there is something about the situation, the customer, or our own state of mind that might otherwise lead us to offer something less than our best.

Humility...the secret sauce to great service.

And the best news of all is my friend recovered from that gunshot injury, has since welcomed another child to the family, and now travels around speaking to groups, letting them know that they too can overcome adversity. What an amazing human being!

Thanks for reading. Thanks for your service.

Be great!

Made in the USA
Columbia, SC
01 July 2024

37833990R00114